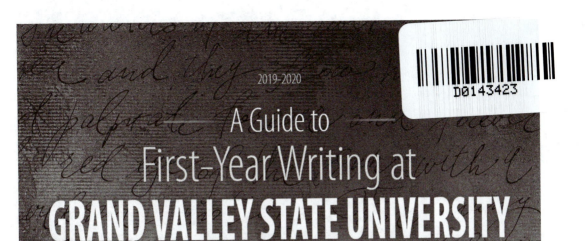

2019-2020

A Guide to
First-Year Writing at
GRAND VALLEY STATE UNIVERSITY

Edited by
SARAH DICKERSON ▪ **CRAIG HULST** ▪ **SARAH SLACHTER**
AMY FERDINANDT STOLLEY ▪ **GALE THOMPSON**

Kendall Hunt
publishing company

www.kendallhunt.com
Send all inquiries to:
4050 Westmark Drive
Dubuque, IA 52004-1840

Copyright ©2017, 2018 by Grand Valley State University

ISBN: 978-1-5249-9431-0

Published in the United States of America

CONTENTS

INTRODUCTION

The first-year writing courses offered by the Department of Writing at Grand Valley State University are designed to build on and expand your writing, critical thinking, collaboration, and information literacy skills. This book, *A Guide to First-Year Writing at Grand Valley State University,* is meant to do just that—*guide* you in this class. (From here on, we will just call this book the Guide.) As a community of writers, we have worked to create a Guide that invites you into our community and celebrates student writing at all stages. We hope you will make extensive use of this Guide, both in class and on your own, to succeed in our required first-year writing course, Writing 150 ("WRT 150" in the Grand Valley catalog).

Our Department of Writing strives to create a consistent program for all students who take WRT 150. Our professors teach WRT 150 using their own preferred teaching methods, but important elements remain consistent across all sections, such as learning outcomes, grading criteria, grading methods, and departmental policies, all of which you will find explained in this book. Each semester every WRT 150 instructor meets once a week with other instructors to discuss these course goals and expectations as they apply to particular students' papers. At the end of the term, these groups of instructors read final portfolios of the work that students produce in WRT 150 and assign each portfolio a grade. As a result, at Grand Valley, you can compare your grade at the end of your first-year writing experience fairly with the grade of every other student on campus who has taken WRT 150.

This Guide tells you more about our shared course expectations for WRT 150. To start, we provide brief descriptions of the other courses that you might take before taking WRT 150, just in case you wish to reconsider your choice of the right place to start your college writing experience. Then we provide a much more detailed guide to WRT 150. First, we provide an overview of WRT 150 so you know the goals we have set out for your learning. Next, we explore the key principles of how and why we write in college that will shape the work you do in WRT 150, which is followed by the University and Writing Department policies that apply to this course. The next section focuses on the WRT 150 portfolio, where we outline our grading policies, submission guidelines, and responses to questions many students enrolled in the course ask. We then provide resources that are available for all student writers at Grand Valley, but that are particularly useful for students enrolled in WRT 150. Finally, you'll find several examples of writing completed in WRT 150 last year that earned As, including entire portfolios and some single standout essays. You will use these samples of student writing to guide your revisions and spur classroom discussion of the grading expectations.

You'll also find some advice from students who have taken WRT 150 in the past. You'll see quotes from Professor Aiman Mueller's students throughout the first part of the book, and before each portfolio, you'll hear about the writers' experiences taking WRT 150 and advice for you as you start this semester. We share it with you here because we think their advice will be helpful, though we're sure you'll come up with your own words of wisdom to share at the end of the semester, too.

FIRST-YEAR WRITING COURSE OPTIONS

As you know by now, you decide which writing course you should take first at Grand Valley after considering information about our departmental requirements and consulting with advisors during orientation. You have these three choices:

► ESL 098 is for second-language students making a transition to standard written English.

► WRT 098 is for students who need more practice and instruction to develop fluency and fullness in their writing.

► WRT 150 is for students who write fluently and are ready to begin college-level academic writing, including writing with sources.

About 85% of students who enter Grand Valley place themselves into WRT 150. If you are reading this Guide, you have already made that choice. Just in case you would like to consider your choice one more time, here are brief descriptions of your other options. If you have doubts about the course you have chosen, talk about your concerns with your professor as soon as possible. Your professor may also assign a quick writing task during the first week of the course, in part to help you make that decision.

ESL 098

Specialists in second language learning teach ESL 098, offered by the Department of English. It is the best starting place for students for whom the English language provides more difficulty than writing itself. In particular, students who are successful writers in another language but who have difficulty writing in English should take ESL 098 rather than WRT 098.

WRT 098

WRT 098 focuses on raising students' confidence in their writing, assisting them in gaining agency and control over their writing and education, and encouraging them to value a lifelong engagement with writing and reading. Students write to learn as well as to communicate, and they learn more about the practice of writing, particularly writing in college. The course invites spontaneity and discovery, seeking to develop in students the kinds of habits and writing strategies that will enable them to succeed in WRT 150 and beyond.

WRT 098 emphasizes immersion, invention, and revision. Students write continually, generating new drafts all semester long. Students learn invention strategies to get papers started, learn to keep the writing process going to produce a substantial volume of writing, and develop positive attitudes toward writing. WRT 098 features peer workshop groups led by trained writing consultants from The Fred Meijer Center for Writing (the "Writing Center"), so that students learn not only the benefits of seeking assistance from the Writing Center, but also the value of thoughtful peer review.

Students in WRT 098 receive a preliminary introduction to college-level research skills, using the Internet and the more advanced research materials available through Grand Valley's library and the library's online resources. WRT 098 also introduces students to using computers in ways that WRT 150 will require. Students who need more help with these more technical aspects of college writing may also want to start in WRT 098.

OVERVIEW OF WRT 150

As the single writing course required of all Grand Valley students, WRT 150 focuses on academic writing, including writing informed by scholarly research. Instructors assume that you are ready to read, summarize, and analyze a wide variety of college-level published material. They also assume that you have experience with narrative, descriptive, and argumentative writing. In most WRT 150 classes, you first write four or five papers, at least one of which integrates material from highly credible sources that you find in the course of doing significant academic research. In most cases, these papers will be four to eight pages long in normal academic format. From among these papers, you will pick three, including at least one that demonstrates your ability to find and integrate source material effectively, to include in your final portfolio for grading. Then, you will spend a considerable amount of time revising and improving your three portfolio papers.

In WRT 150, you encounter challenging reading material—whether you find it in assigned readings or in your own research materials—and you practice discussing, summarizing, and analyzing that material. You also work on improving writing processes that can help you complete new kinds of writing tasks and rise to new levels of writing ability—processes that move effectively from prewriting, inventing, planning, and drafting to revising, consulting, editing, and finishing.

In most sections, half of your WRT 150 class meetings take place in a computer classroom. Each computer is connected to the Internet and the Grand Valley network. The Grand Valley network includes personal storage space on the campus server and special access to research sources maintained by Grand Valley's library system. WRT 150 instructors assume that you have a basic familiarity with computers, word processors, Web browsers, and e-mail.

By the end of WRT 150, as an experienced college writer you should be able to:

Prewrite, Invent, and Plan

▶ Read and understand material written for college audiences.

▶ Develop clearly focused written summaries, analyses, and paraphrases that demonstrate an understanding of the material you have read.

▶ Develop ideas using a variety of prewriting techniques, which may include brainstorming, freewriting, journal-keeping, consulting with others, conducting library research, and analyzing your audiences.

Revise, Develop, and Shape

▶ Develop writing from early, writer-oriented drafts to later, reader-oriented drafts.

▶ Produce effective writing for a variety of purposes, such as narrating, explaining, exploring, and persuading.

▶ Demonstrate the ability to focus your writing on supportable themes, claims, or theories.

▶ Support your focus using well-selected details that are accurate and relevant.

▶ Consult with peer reviewers and other readers to assess the further needs of your drafts.

▶ Revise writing with particular audiences in mind, including academic audiences.

▶ Conduct effective, significant scholarly research.

▶ Integrate facts and opinions from a variety of sources into your own writing.

Refine, Edit, and Finish

► Include words, facts, and ideas from research sources in ways that fully credit the original source and avoid plagiarism.
► Control the main features of a specific documentation style (like MLA or APA).
► Refine your sentence structures to produce an effective style and voice.
► Edit writing so that academic audiences can read the writing without having their attention and understanding diverted by problems in grammar, spelling, punctuation, and format.

In addition to requiring WRT 150, Grand Valley supports the development of your writing ability in other courses. Many General Education courses also focus on developing your writing in specific academic areas. After building that foundation, you will take two courses in disciplines of interest to you specifically designated as Supplemental Writing Skills courses. You may also take further writing courses, and many of your college courses will involve extensive writing. Thus, WRT 150 is not the end of your college writing instruction. Instead, it seeks to supply you with an important foundation that you will build on for the rest of your college career.

> *"Do not be afraid of writing. Don't take so much time to plan how to make the perfect essay; just write and be willing to revise."*
> —Brendan K.

Finally, WRT 150 is also part of your General Education Foundation, and like all General Education courses, we work to improve intellectual skills that you will use in later courses and in your life after college. In WRT 150, we focus mainly on improving your skill in Written Communication, but we also strive to work explicitly on your Information Literacy skills. Throughout the semester, your instructor should assign and provide feedback on activities related to your ability to identify, evaluate, and work with different forms of information.

WRT 150 GOALS

By the end of WRT 150, your final portfolio should demonstrate that you have achieved the program's goals and can perform each of these tasks:

Content and Development

▶ Offer readers a clear purpose for reading.

▶ Maintain a single focus throughout the entire paper.

▶ Present ideas and descriptions that engage a college-level audience in your discussion.

▶ Conduct college-level research to find credible source material for a variety of purposes.

▶ Present a claim or focus that is developed with discussion, details, and examples, including graphics when useful.

▶ Discover and integrate sufficient material from outside sources to demonstrate your abilities in college level writing, research, and thinking.

Organization

▶ Establish an overall pattern for a paper to follow.

▶ Progress from one point, idea, or scene to another in a coherent, logical way.

▶ Construct paragraphs that are generally well-organized within the overall pattern of a paper.

▶ Lead readers through the order of your discussion in obvious and helpful ways.

Style

▶ Craft sentences with purposefully chosen words and phrases.

▶ Structure sentences effectively to be clear, logical, and readable.

▶ Use a variety of sentence structures for good reasons.

▶ Maintain an overall voice in each paper that is appropriate for its purpose, genre, and audiences.

Mechanics

▶ Adopt a format that is acceptable and appropriate for academic writing.

▶ Refer to outside sources that are introduced, integrated, and documented.

▶ Attend carefully to grammar, spelling, punctuation, and usage in final, edited writing.

▶ Use with care a standard academic style guide, such as the MLA or APA style guides.

HOW AND WHY WE WRITE

WRITING AS A PROCESS

When we think of writers, we might imagine people who possess some magical talent that allows them to sit down and instantly transfer their thoughts onto paper. But researchers have concluded that expert writers do not simply sit down and "put it in writing" in one easy step. Rather, successful experienced writers work through a complex process to get to their final product. Different writers follow different steps in that process depending on their needs and personal preferences, but in general, expert writers experience writing as a process that unfolds over time, not as a "one and done" burst of inspiration.

For instance, when faced with the need to communicate to an audience, experienced writers begin by exploring their own knowledge, feelings, and beliefs; considering the knowledge, feelings, and beliefs of their intended readers; and searching for something specific that needs to be said. Then they explore their communication options—the various forms available to them—before sketching out, reconsidering, revising, and polishing their message, making sure they are sensitive to their readers. Often, at several points during the writing process, expert writers ask friends or peers—people no more expert than they are, and often less so—to take a look at their drafted material and give advice or feedback. Finally, when satisfied with their efforts, expert writers polish the results and deliver their writing to their intended audience.

The example above illustrates five basic parts of a successful writing process:

- ► **Prewriting and Inventing**: generating ideas; forming questions for investigation and constructing a research plan; collecting, evaluating, and managing information; identifying possible subjects, purposes, audiences, and forms.

- ► **Planning and Drafting**: trying out ideas and approaches; zeroing in on a single focus and a single form.

- ► **Consulting**: talking with people about preliminary ideas, plans, and drafts; soliciting oral and written feedback from friends and colleagues about content, structure, audience appeal, style, and correctness.

- ► **Revising and Shaping**: considering additions and deletions; reshaping and refocusing existing material; and editing for style, flow, and obvious error.

- ► **Editing and Finishing**: taking authorial responsibility for the final product; editing carefully for correctness and format; and delivering the final product to its intended audience (instructor, relative, client, committee, editor, etc.).

Although the list above outlines the steps expert writers take as they complete writing projects, it is important to note that they don't always happen in order. There is no "correct" writing process. Some writers may follow the steps in order, but others might start with consulting, move on to drafting, and then work on invention activities to help generate new ideas or an organizational structure for the essay. Over the course of the semester, you'll find the process and strategies that work best for *you* as a writer, and you can apply those strategies to other writing tasks you'll encounter as a student and in the workplace.

Developing Your Writing Process with New Strategies

While you will probably have a unique way of going through the steps set out above, at some point all expert writers need to find ways of addressing the concerns of each step effectively. As instructors of WRT 150, we are not merely judges of your writing. In fact, you might best view instructors as coaches whose primary goal is to help you develop processes that you will use for the writing you do in WRT 150, in future Grand Valley classes, and on the job. We help you explore your writing processes through class information, class discussions, stimulating writing assignments, and responses to your writing in progress.

Your instructor will help you explore your writing processes, but you can take control of your own processes by considering the following checklist that we have devised to help you develop expert methods. You don't need to do all of the strategies listed here, but we encourage you to try a few in each category and reflect on how it changes and improves your writing process.

> *"Work on small amounts every day, whether it's just writing one paragraph, finding one source, or coming up with a single idea."*
>
> *—Philip B.*

Prewriting and Inventing

- ▶ Use a variety of brainstorming techniques to generate, develop, and focus topics.
- ▶ Write informally in journals or notebooks as an ongoing writer's activity.
- ▶ Use writing as a tool for learning as well as communicating.
- ▶ Analyze audience as a method of planning and focusing.
- ▶ Consider purpose, style, and form in relation to audience during the planning stages.
- ▶ Weigh a variety of form and style options during the planning stages.
- ▶ Sequence and initiate your own writing process to suit immediate purposes.
- ▶ Generate and select your own methods for developing material.
- ▶ Engage in prewriting discussions with your instructor and peers.
- ▶ Read as a writer; read published materials critically.
- ▶ Write and speak about yourself as a writer.
- ▶ Form questions for investigation and construct a research plan.
- ▶ Collect, evaluate, and manage information.

- Use basic reference materials (dictionary, encyclopedia, online search engine).
- Use research as a form of generating ideas and planning writing.
- Consider how numerical and graphic information or images might support your focus and purpose.

Planning and Drafting

- Translate prewriting activities into drafts.
- Adapt your writing for specific readers, including academic ones.
- Write for broad, public, academic audiences.
- Vary diction and tone according to audience.
- Establish and maintain a focus that has a purpose.
- Maintain a consistent style throughout the different parts.
- Cultivate an appropriate and interesting voice.
- Integrate ideas and information from outside sources.
- Support ideas and observations with details, including numerical and graphic information and images.
- Save different drafts with different file names when you make important changes.

Consulting

- Use feedback from peers.
- Give feedback to peers.
- Engage in revision discussions with your instructor, peers, and writing consultant.
- Survey and integrate readers' needs and interests.
- Write alternate and more fully realized new versions of earlier drafts.
- Work productively in writing groups.

Revising and Shaping

- Write and use your own evaluations of your drafts.
- Adapt the style and voice of your language to suit your purpose and audience.

- ▶ Revise for focus, development, order, structure, balance, and emphasis.
- ▶ Align the information and reasoning in the paper with the paper's focus.
- ▶ Add, delete, change, or recast material to suit your purposes and readers.
- ▶ Establish a clear focus throughout the paper.
- ▶ Consider the wide variety of readers for whom you might actually be writing.
- ▶ Revise paragraphing and sentences for greater clarity and interest.
- ▶ Achieve "closure" in later drafts; make sure the product can become a consistent whole work.

Editing and Finishing

- ▶ Proofread all writing intended for public audiences.
- ▶ Use your word processor's editing software to help you spot possible areas for improvement.
- ▶ Refresh your editing eye and ear by using methods like reading aloud, reading sentences in reverse order, reading as if you were somebody else (like your favorite Uncle or Aunt), or putting the latest draft away for a day or two.
- ▶ Use a dictionary and handbook for editing.
- ▶ Check your documentation with a guide for your documentation style.
- ▶ Check your use of material from sources to be sure you are using source material ethically.

Responding to Peer Writing

Most instructors have students offer valuable feedback on each other's papers for two good reasons. Peer review will give you valuable feedback from peers to help you improve your drafts to help you think critically about your writing. You'll also get the chance to see how your classmates responded to the same assignment prompt you did, which can help generate ideas for how you might revise or refocus your own essay. We encourage students to practice peer review on their own, outside of class. As you practice peer

> *"Don't tell yourself that you can't write something. You may not think you're creative, but you are . . . Write as frequently as you can. Write and revise. Let others see your writing. Know how to use feedback. Let others know that you appreciate their feedback."*
>
> — *Tim H.*

review, you should avoid closing the door with final negative or positive evaluations on students' papers. If you judge early drafts by saying "your opening is perfect" or "this is already an A paper," you encourage your peers to stop rethinking and rewriting their papers. That might feel good for a moment, but it will not help anyone to improve.

Your instructor will probably have many suggestions about how to do successful peer reviews. Generally, experts in writing say to focus on global issues before moving on to local issues. Global revision means seeing the "big picture" and focusing on organization, and development of ideas, audience, and tone. Local revision means paying attention to details and focusing on editing for word choice, sentence fluency, grammar, spelling, and punctuation.

INFORMATION LITERACY AND ACADEMIC CONVERSATIONS

As academic writers, we work in a world of information and opinion, so it is very common for us to refer to facts and ideas originally published in other sources, and then to quote and cite those sources in ways that carefully show where we got our information. Educators commonly refer to this ability as "information literacy," and it's a skill that is valued highly in universities across the country, including GVSU.

Information literacy is a crucial skill in your development as a writer because it offers you strategies for participating in academic conversations. That may sound like a strange phrase—academic conversations—and it might evoke images of tweed-wearing professors debating obscure points of philosophy. While that might still happen somewhere, most academic conversations today are conducted in the writing of academic papers. In writing studies, we often refer to academic writing as a conversation because a good writer is in *dialogue* with the sources he or she chooses to integrate into the essay. A writer might agree with a source and use it to verify the argument he or she is making, or a writer might disagree with a source but still use its ideas as a springboard for making his/her own argument. Either way, when writers engage with sources and incorporate them into their writing, they are participating in an ongoing conversation with writers and thinkers engaged and interested in a specific issue, and they use their information literacy skills to do so.

We focus on information literacy in WRT 150 for three main reasons. First, we want readers to take our writing seriously because we have done our homework, so to speak, by taking the time to find out what the credible authorities on the subject have already said. Second, we want our readers to understand how our own ideas relate to those of credible experts. Third, we want to give proper credit to those who have already written on the subject; after all, we want credit for our own work, so we afford others the same courtesy. Together, these three goals help us to accomplish our larger goal of participating in ongoing scholarly and expert conversations—which is really what research writing does, at its best.

Doing that work well starts with doing excellent research—going beyond the world of mere opinions that are so easily available on the Internet and learning how to find, read, and use the kind of information on which experts rely.

Research is a key step in any writer's process, and it's one that can strongly influence the outcome of your final product. Grand Valley's expert research librarians have developed "Information Literacy Core Competencies" (ILCCs) for college students, defining six main goals for college-level research. According to the ILCCs, as a college-level researcher, you should learn to:

- ► construct a question or problem statement,
- ► locate and gather information,
- ► evaluate sources,
- ► manage information,
- ► use information ethically, and
- ► communicate knowledge.

You will develop these abilities throughout your college career, but WRT 150 will give a strong foundation in all these areas. In WRT

150 you will learn to *construct research questions* to develop a preliminary focus to help you manage the range of material that you might pursue. You will learn to *create a plan* for your search for information and identify the resources that will be available to help you (such as library guides, access to scholarly journals through online reference tools called databases, and the research librarians themselves). You will learn to *evaluate sources* so that you use the most appropriate and effective information rather than just the materials that pop up first in a Web search. You will learn to *manage information* in ways that help you keep track of what you have found and lower the stress and anxiety of conducting complicated research. Of course, as we reemphasize in many ways in this Guide, you will learn to *use information ethically* by giving other writers credit for what you have learned from them and for what they have written. By learning to cite sources correctly, you learn to avoid plagiarism, honor copyright, and participate expertly in academic discussions. Finally, we want you to *communicate knowledge* effectively by coming to understand how those academic discussions take place, and then by participating in those discussions.

We cannot overemphasize the importance of these information literacy competencies as part of an effective academic writing process. Information literacy does not always show up directly in grading criteria because it is essentially a process, not a product; yet information literacy will have a profound effect on your ability to communicate your ideas to an audience effectively.

Sources and Evidence

When we talk about information literacy in WRT 150, we pay attention to the types of sources and types of evidence that students use to support their discussions about the topics they choose. In your previous writing classes, much of your research was probably done with Google—finding online sources that prove the point you want to make (or maybe help you figure out what you want your point to be). While those are certainly valid sources and can be part of the research you conduct in WRT 150, your instructor will work with you to use library resources to find deeper and more complex credible sources that are the hallmark of academic writing and conversations. Your instructor will teach you strategies for determining if a source is credible, and he or she may have specific guidelines for the types of sources you are expected to use in your essays. Generally speaking, though, you can expect to learn how to find, integrate, and cite the following types of sources into your own writing (though you are certainly not limited to this list):

- ► Scholarly sources from peer-reviewed journals, including reports of scientific studies, experiments, or qualitative research (interviews, case studies, etc.)
- ► Scholarly or popular press books
- ► News reports from reputable journalism publications
- ► Analytical articles or essays from reputable journalism publications
- ► US Government reports, studies, or laws
- ► Organization Web sites devoted to specific social, political, or health issues (e.g., Bill and Melinda Gates Foundation, American Heart Association)
- ► TED Talks delivered by experts or other documentary films or videos

Academic writers use many different types of sources including those above, but it's important to remember that expert writers use research to provide different types of information and evidence that they find from these sources. Often, WRT 150 students assume that when their instructors ask them to incorporate research into their essays, the instructors are looking for statistics. Sometimes statistics help develop a writer's essay, but sources can be used to provide different types of evidence that advance a writer's purpose in meaningful ways. Therefore, we encourage WRT 150 students to think broadly about the types of information that reliable sources can offer. For example, a student who was writing an essay exploring how workers are affected by automation (using robots and computers to complete tasks originally done by humans), could use a range of types of evidence to support the discussion as shown below:

Types of Evidence	Examples
Facts or statistics	▶ Identifying number of people laid off by automation in the last decade ▶ Citing the number of companies/industries that have shifted to automation in the last decade ▶ Quoting government unemployment statistics due to automation
Anecdotes	▶ Describing the experiences of individuals who lost their jobs because their companies/factories shifted to automation models of production ▶ Quoting company officials explaining why they made the move to automation
Analogies	▶ Comparing how workers in other countries have been affected by automation ▶ Comparing current automation trends to the effect of industrialization (such as in the auto industry) during the early twentieth century
Scientific study report	▶ Explaining a study that examined the relationship between automation and unemployment ▶ Summarizing a study of a company that chose not to automate to understand how such a trend influences workers and company profits
Expert testimonial	▶ Citing opinions or arguments from leading economists who study the effects of automation on labor markets and unemployment ▶ Quoting psychologists who study the impact of job loss on workers who were laid off because their jobs were no longer needed

Although it would make sense for a writer to include statistical information or facts in an essay about automation and unemployment, it's clear that different types of evidence would add nuance, detail, and complexity to the writer's discussion of the topic. When you review the student writing in the Guide, pay attention not just to the types of sources that students used, but also *how* they used them. You'll see a range of sources used for a variety of purposes, and we encourage you to work toward that in your own writing, as well.

The benefits of information literacy go well beyond WRT 150. When you learn to include results from research into your writing effectively, you prepare yourself for success in later college work. Making good decisions about the sources you wish to cite and how that information helps you to accomplish your writing purpose helps you to be in control of your writing. Summarizing, para-phrasing, and quoting your sources effectively shows that you truly understand them. Citing and documenting your sources correctly proves not only that you understand your sources but also that you understand how academic writing works. It also helps you to avoid charges of plagiarism. When we work with sources, we have to take special care to make sure that readers know exactly what we are claiming as our own thinking and writing and exactly what came from someone else. We will resist discussing research, documenta-tion, and plagiarism at great length here because all of that needs to be addressed far more extensively in your WRT 150 class. You must, however, be alert to the importance of using research mate-rial ethically in WRT 150 and throughout your college career.

DOCUMENTING SOURCES

We have referred above to "documentation" of sources, which may be a new term for you. Basically, documentation means giving readers a very precise way to know exactly where you got your lan-guage and information and when exactly you are using language or information from your sources. For example, you might have seen books that had footnotes at the bottom of the page, linked to small numbers inserted into the discussion. Those footnotes "document" the source of the information.

To make that reference work easier to do, academic writers have created several carefully defined documentation styles, depending on the field or discipline in which they are writing. In the same way that there are (sometimes unstated) rules associated with texting or tweeting, scholars have developed rules about how academic conversations are conducted through writing, and these rules are articulated by documentation styles. Most writers in the humanities use the documen-tation system of the Modern Language Associa-tion (MLA style), and this is the documentation style used most often in WRT 150 classes. Writ-ers in the social sciences usually use the docu-mentation system of the American Psychological Association (APA style), so some WRT 150 classes use, or at least permit, APA style. Both of these styles insert a brief citation to a source inside

"Working on a works cited as you go along instead of all at the end like I did would be easier."

—Sammy M.

parentheses (often starting with an author's last name) within the body of an essay, and then add a list of sources at the end that readers can identify quickly by using the information in the parentheses. All of the sample essays in this book that cite sources use those documentation styles. If you have not worked with documentation very much, be sure to look at those examples so that you have a better idea of how they work.

You will likely learn several documentation styles during your college career. We understand that this variety of documentation styles can seem confusing, but please try to keep an open mind about them. By the time you are done with college, you will settle into some familiar styles for your work, and you will come to understand all the problems these documentation styles actually solve for you. There are good reasons for the differences between documentation styles, rooted in disciplinary practices and priorities. For now, you mainly need to remember that they are meant to be used precisely, and that their accurate use is your best method to avoid charges of plagiarism.

AVOIDING PLAGIARISM

Certainly, you understand that you cannot have someone else do your writing for you or copy a paper and turn it in as your own. Most students also understand Grand Valley's policy forbidding submission of the same work in two different classes (including earlier high school classes)—unless you have permission from *both* instructors. Many first-year college students believe that as long as they avoid such extremely dishonest behavior, they cannot be accused of plagiarism; unfortunately, that belief is not correct.

Plagiarism is not simply a matter of dishonest intentions. Working with research sources requires writers to understand difficult aspects of plagiarism and make skilled, positive efforts to credit sources accurately and fully. Again, everyone knows that you cannot use the words of other writers without putting those words in quotation marks and giving the original writer credit. Many first-year students are surprised to find that, to avoid committing plagiarism, they also must do the following:

- ▶ Give credit to sources for their *information and ideas* as well as their words;
- ▶ Quote any exact language from the source, even only a few words at a time, when they use that language within their own sentences;
- ▶ Avoid using the same general sentence structure used by the source, except in exact and clearly marked quotations;
- ▶ Use their documentation style precisely to make perfectly clear when they are using material from a source and when they are presenting their own words and ideas.

You will learn more about documentation and avoiding plagiarism throughout WRT 150, so your instructor may continue to work with your drafts even if they contain sections that might commit intentional or unintentional plagiarism. If you want more information about why we do that, read the statement by the national Council of Writing Program Administrators (CWPA) about best approaches to working with students on the concept of plagiarism, found online at http://www.wpacouncil.org/positions/WPAplagiarism.pdf.

Furthermore, we may not always see when you are using material from sources while we are working on your drafts. We rely on you to inform us of that. Nevertheless, by the end of the course, in your final portfolio, we will check closely for plagiarism and hold you entirely accountable for it according to the Grand Valley Student Code. Thus, you need to be sure that you understand how to document all your sources before the end of WRT 150. Be sure that you ask your instructor or consultants in the Writing Center about any instances of possible plagiarism in your work.

FOCUSING ON REVISION: ONE STUDENT'S PROCESS

One of the most important skills you will practice and develop in WRT 150 this semester is your ability to revise your own writing. Revision is difficult—once we do the hard work of getting our ideas onto the page, it can be painful to change it, move it around, or worse, delete it. A novice writer is more likely to simply correct a few sentence-level errors and then call revision done; however, a more experienced writer knows that careful revision requires one to take a step back from the draft, look at the big picture, and ask important questions about purpose, audience, organization, and clarity. These questions might change the essay radically, but more often than not, the change is for the better because it helps the writer think more clearly about what the writer wants to communicate to the audience.

To help illustrate the types of radical revisions students do in WRT 150, we've selected an essay that Anna Wheeler wrote in Professor Stolley's class. Rather than showing you only the final product that Anna turned in at the end of the semester, we've collected two of her earlier drafts to show how her essay changed—and improved significantly—through revision. A marketing and human resources management major from Sparta, MI, Anna says that she's most proud of this essay, "The 'Wrong Kind' of Asian." The essay explores stereotypes against Asian Americans, and according to Anna, writing it allowed her to research and become more comfortable talking about her own experience and perspective as an Asian American with others.

Anna's first draft is a two-page exploration of her topic, and you'll see how her focus and purpose change as she continues writing, researching, and revising in subsequent drafts. You'll also see in her revised draft that she included notes to herself about ideas she knew she needed to develop and revise in further drafts. As we stated earlier, each writer's process is different, so we don't expect you all to follow Anna's exact model. However, by viewing this example, we think you and your classmates will be able to point out the specific revision strategies Anna used so that you might try them out in your own writing this semester.

Anna's Advice for WRT 150 Students

I believe students often get frustrated with finding a topic because they think their lives are "boring" and/or "not interesting enough." This is not true. Finding topics to write about is not easy, especially personal related ones. My advice is to find something that you consider a personal victory. No matter how small the accomplishment is, it could lead to a spark of new ideas. Another idea is to find something that has always bothered you. Jot down all of your feelings towards the topic and then go back and research to find more issues related to the topic. You will find much more information and learn that you are not alone on the idea.

ANNA'S FIRST DRAFT

The "Wrong Kind" of Asian

It seems that today, we are all assigned a label. This label is something we carry around with us for the rest of our lives. Many of us are often unhappy with the label we are given, and strive to change it throughout our times Due to my ethnicity, I have been labeled a "typical Asian" by my small community of prevalently white-race. When I step into bigger communities such as Grand Valley State University, the stereotype still follows me, wherever I go. The typical Asian stereotype seem to be stamped onto my forehead. Even though I was adopted by a white family, people continue to judge me off my looks. People assume several things about me, such as my smartness, my language I speak, and my economic success, all due to my looks. This stereotype comes from the "Model Minority" representation of Asian Americans, where their demographic profile speaks for the whole group. According to Taylor and Stern, Asian Americans are considered a "model minority" due to their affluence, high education, and managerial/ professional occupations- and rapid growth in number. The Model Minority theory ultimately dismantles Asians leaving them behind with a preconceived way of how they must function in life and provokes discriminating and racist behavior.

Similar to all other racial stereotypes, Asian Americans are subjected to a variety of stereotypes. Racial slang is often thrown in my face on the daily, yet sometimes I wonder where people are attaining their information from and if they fully understand what they are saying. Several of the Asian stereotypes that can used today, correlate with the events that have happened in the past. The Immigration Act of 1965, welcomed large numbers of Asians to enter the United States to work. Prior to this act, immigration into the US was regulated by the National Origins system, which "limited immigration from Asian to token levels" ("The 1965"). The new Immigration Act abolished restrictive quotas and relaxed the preference system. However, it only provided mass entry for those who fit the certain classes required of Asians. The requirement only allowed the wealthiest and educated from each Asian country into the US. After immigrating the certain classes, several professionals, scientists, technicians, graduate students, etc., where recruited to immigrate to the US. Policymakers sought this plan in order to fill scientific and technical positions that American students could not successfully fill. As a result, the immigration policy "controlled the quality of Asian immigrants in ways that they did not for other minorities" (Yen, 3). Thus, the inundation of successful Asians into America all at one time created a change in character for the Asian community, who were once viewed as "Yellow Peril", Asians viewed as aliens and a threat to wage-earners already in the US.

The emergence of the post-1965 Asian immigrants led to tensions between the old-time residents (US-born) and the new immigrated minority groups. The US-born citizens of the time accused many Asians of taking over and exploiting their communities. Several of the second-generation Asian Americans began working with the successful white Americans, which curated the white Americans ideas of Asian Americans as The Model Minority. The term "model minority" was first introduced in January 1966 in a New York Times Magazine by sociologist William Petersen. In his article, "Success story: Japanese American Style", the success of Japanese American is "quickly generalized across all Asian ethnic groups, regardless of their diversity in culture, education, and class" (Yoo). The success of appraised newly immigrated Asians appeared in numerous press articles. However, the Immigration Act of 1965 was often overlooked in Petersen's coining of "model minority". The lifting of restrictions and recruiting of professionals, is what ultimately created the large influx of successful Asian Americans. Petersen's term also concealed the discrepancies of other concepts, such as income, education, and health. The model minority term has led to the stereotyping of Asians that is now affecting current generations.

Paragraph 4—effects on communities
The Model Minority stereotype is proof that some racial stereotypes can seem favorable, however the people of the group can also be exploited in negative way. The model-minority image brings about a number of problems.

Paragraph 5—effects on communities
Paragraph 6—how it can be proven wrong
Paragraph 7—conclusion

Word Count: 712

ANNA'S REVISED DRAFT

The "Wrong Kind" of Asian

I am Asian. Growing up in a Caucasian-populated town, I am an easy target for bullies. I am always the odd one out. My outward appearances do not look like everyone else's. Not everyone accepts my nationality, but I am proud of it. As a young child, I never considered myself "different" from everyone else. My parents are both white. While I was growing up, they have always made me feel like I belonged. My point-of-view was changed when someone pointed out to me that I was different from everyone else. "Your eyes look different than mine" is the statement that started it all and still continues to be pointed out to me. I remember going home that night and wondering why my eyes were different from everyone else's. This was something I pondered over for several years. Why couldn't I just look like everyone else?

Racism isn't just black and white. The racist jokes I receive are usually all the same: "Open your eyes," "Go back to the rice picking fields," "You have to be smart... You're Asian." These stereotypes comes from the "Model Minority" representation of Asian Americans, where their demographic profile speaks for the whole group. According to Taylor and Stern, Asian Americans are considered a "model minority" due to their affluence, high education, and managerial/professional occupations- and rapid growth in number. The Model Minority theory leaves Asians behind with a preconceived way of how they must function in life and provokes discriminating and racist behavior.

Similar to all other racial stereotypes, Asian Americans are subjected to a variety of stereotypes. Racial slang is often thrown in my face on the daily, yet sometimes I wonder where people are attaining their information from and if they fully understand what they are saying. Several of the Asian stereotypes that can used today, correlate with the events that have happened in the past. The Immigration Act of 1965 welcomed large numbers of Asians to enter the United States to work. Prior to this act, immigration into the US was regulated by the National Origins system, which "limited immigration from Asian to token levels" ("The 1965"). The new Immigration Act abolished restrictive quotas and relaxed the preference system. However, it only provided mass entry for those who fit the certain classes required of Asians. The requirement only allowed the wealthiest and educated from each Asian country into the US. After immigrating, the certain classes, several professionals, scientists, technicians, graduate students, and others were recruited to immigrate to the US. Policymakers sought this plan in order to fill scientific and technical positions that American students could not successfully fill. As a result, the immigration policy "controlled the quality of Asian immigrants in ways that they did not for other minorities" (Yen 3). Thus, the inundation of successful Asians into America all at one time created a change in character for the Asian community, who were once viewed as "Yellow Peril", aliens and a threat to wage-earners already in the US.

The emergence of the post-1965 Asian immigrants led to tensions between the old-time residents (US-born) and the new immigrated minority groups. The US-born citizens of the time accused many Asians of taking over and exploiting their communities. Several of the second-generation Asian Americans began working with the successful white Americans, which curated the white Americans ideas of Asian Americans as The Model Minority. The term "model minority" was first introduced in January 1966 in a New York Times Magazine by sociologist William Petersen. In his article, "Success Story: Japanese American Style", the success of Japanese Americans is emphasized upon because _____ (Japanese were believed to be the clostest to Americans); thus, he "quickly generalized across all Asian ethnic groups, regardless of their diversity in culture, education, and class" (Yoo). The success of newly immigrated Asians appeared in numerous press articles. However, the Immigration Act of 1965 was often overlooked in Petersen's coining of "model minority". The lifting of restrictions and recruiting of professionals is what ultimately created the large influx of successful Asian Americans. Petersen's term also concealed the discrepancies of other concepts, such as income, education, and health. The model minority term has led to the stereotyping of Asians that is now affecting current generations.

The Model Minority stereotype is proof that some racial stereotypes can seem favorable, however the people of the group can also be exploited in negative way. The model-minority image brings about several problems. One of the major implications that arise is harsh stereotyping and discrimination. The way the media portrays the Asian American community encourages others to participate in the "typical Asian" stereotyping that leads to perceptions that all members of the community are alike. When ABC debuted its new sitcom in 2015 titled, Fresh Off the Boat, which featured an Asian American family, the cast was asked an offensive question during its open panel. The panel was asked "from an unknown reporter who said, 'I love the Asian culture. And I was just talking about the chopsticks, and I just love all that. Will I get to see that, or will it be more Americanized?'" (McRady). This goes to prove that the so called "outdated" stereotypes still exist and are repulsive throughout the media. The reporter ultimately reduced the entire Asian culture to chopsticks. Although much of the stereotyping of Asians are positive, they can still lead to several factors that ultimately leave the Asian community at disadvantage. A study was conducted that focused on Asian-American's participants ethnicity and was hypothesized to make them derive better test scores than those participants whose identities were not identified beforehand. However, the study resulted in, "under these conditions, ethnicity salience resulted in diminished ability to concentrate, which in turn led to significantly impaired math performance" (Cheryan). This research is crucial considering that people hold positive stereotypes over Asians and their mathematical skills. By doing so, this creates high pressure for the Asian community and can result in a negative performance on test.

Additionally, the Model Minority theory forces upon the idea that Asians are not outstanding communicators due to the language barrier and are therefore quiet and silent. However, this is affecting several Asian Americans and Pacific Islanders students in the classroom as this stereotypical image "may also pose pressure upon them to violate their cultural upbringing and conform to the Western norms in the classroom, where grades are often based upon students' verbal participation" (FIND AUTHOR). In result of conforming, this can conflictingly affect the relationship between parent and child of Asian ethnicity. Several Asian families come with their own ethics and morels; the Model Minority theory can put pressure onto young Asian students to change their ways in the classroom to what they were previously raised to do.

The Asian stereotype, mainly driven from the Model Minority Theory, that yet continues to thrive to its existence today, is often ignored because several people (outside of the Asian ethnicity) view the image as something "positive". The typical "smart Asian" stereotype leads everyone to conclude that if you're Asian, you must be smart. In turn, this puts a lot of pressure on Asians who are not "naturally smart" to attempt to live up to their standard or else face outside judgements. Many Asians feel that they are unable to create an image for themselves, but rather already have a template waiting for them to fill. The pressure to fill this template is discussed in Asian American Law Journal. Rhoda J. Yen mentioned Daya Sandhu, a Professsor of Educational and Counseling Psychology who explained that the social pressure to fulfill the "smart Asian" stereotype causes numerous "mental health concerns and psychological afflictions, such as threats to cultural identity, powerlessness, feelings of marginality, loneliness, hostility and perceived alienation and discrimination" (Rhoda). The amount of pressure on Asian Americans that is causing health problems is being hidden under the positive attributes that are ultimately just reinforcing racism.

Note: (use as support- people see Asians as threat, thus the negativity towards them) people often feel realistic threat from groups that are perceived as model minorities such as Asian Americans. In other words, the perception that Asian Americans or other groups have certain model minority traits—including being hardworking, intelligent, and ambitious—leads to a sense that such groups pose a threat to other groups in terms of educational, economic, and political opportunities, and that such a sense of realistic threat may lead to negative attitudes and emotions. (Maddux).

(Option 2- Asian stereotypes being ignored)

They also argued that their experiences of racism and discrimination as a minority were often dismissed, as some people outside the group believed that —Asians are the new Whites [16] (p. 76). This is related to the model minority stereotype, which views AAPIs as privileged and accomplished.

Similarly, the Georgia State University sociologist Rosalind Chou has found that the model-minority standard places enormous pressure on Asian Americans to disavow and downplay incidents of racial harassment; when Asian Americans are depicted as the minority group that doesn't complain, attract negative attention, or cause problems, it can feel uncomfortable for them to point out stereotypes, insults, and assaults. (The Atlantic).

"Asian Americans can also feel embarrassed to acknowledge failure to achieve certain academic or occupational achievements and thus do not seek help" (Zhen).

In addition to receiving racial hinders, Asian Americans are also affected by the Model Minority in institutional organizations such as the workplace and colleges. Although a majority of the Asian community has differing levels of college degrees, many of which are only being used at low-level jobs. An Asian American organization, ASCEND, collected data from HP, Intel, Google, LinkedIn, and Yahoo to show that within these top companies, Asian Americans represent 27% of professionals, 19% of managers, and just 14% of executives" (Chin). It was additionally calculated that "in these five firms, and white men and women are 154% more likely than Asians to hold an executive role" (Johnson). The Model Minority represents Asians as a group of hard working individuals who thrive to be successful and pass the work-ethic drive onto their offspring. The naturally "smart Asian" stereotype mentioned above, tends to follow Asians throughout their life, even in the professional field. So why aren't Asians advancing in the workplace? Jane Hyun explained the situation by coining the term "Bamboo Ceiling", similar to the "Glass Ceiling" effect. This term examines the level of diversity while climbing a corporate ladder. It can be seen in any business; the higher you climb, the less diversity is found. This can revert back to the stereotyping of Asians as poor communicators, which is a big turn off for a leadership position.

Another reason why Asian Americans may not be reaching the leadership spots in the professional workplace is due to college admissions. Much of the Asian population attend Ivy-League schools and elite universities nationwide and are continuing to overtake fields such as medicine, engineering, and computer science. However, their representation at Harvard University is steadily stable, with no increase or decrease. With the increase in population of Asian Americans rising sharply, there was much speculation for why Harvard's count for Asian Americans wasn't increasing. There is much speculation that Harvard has a quota in which they limit their Asian American representation and therefore reject several Asian students despite their top notch performances. According to Strauss, "many Asian-American students who have almost perfect SAT scores, top 1% GPAs, plus significant awards or leadership positions in various extracurricular activities have been rejected by Harvard University". In response, the Asian community filed a complaint against Harvard complaining that they are using racial quotas to admit students other than the Asians. While this is a severe problem, many Asian Americans are choosing to opt around this roadblock to their college admission. Brian Taylor, an Ivy league coach out of Manhattan, is directing his clients to not check "Asian" when applying for colleges as this makes the student appear "less Asian" and therefore appear as just a "normal" smart student. This is creating a strain on Asian students as they have their future to worry for due to their ethnicity.

(Asians in the workplace- less higher up positions due to COLLEGE admissions)

"Since the Ivies produce a disproportionate number of CEOs, Congressmen and judges, the apparent bias against Asian-Americans at leading universities may also keep Asians out of leadership spots. "The ladder is being pulled away from our feet," says Tricia Liu. "If we can't go to the Ivy League universities, how can we get the positions in Wall Street, or Congress, or the Supreme Court?"("Model Minority...")

Despite the Model Minority theory that has wound the world's brain around the stereotypes of Asians, this model seems to be more of a myth than something to follow. The Model Minoirty isolates the Asian populations in a way that can tragically hurt them. It creates high expecatations that can be proven wrong. The Model Minority myth presents Asians as successful in their careers with a financially stable background. When examining the poverty rates in 2007-2011 published by the US Census, Asian Americans ranked one of the lowest poverty rates according to race at 12.8%., with whites ranking comparably (Macartney). However, when looking closer at the data, Asian Americans were experiencing the fastest growth in poverty rates in the United States. According to the Center for American Progress, during the same term of 2007-2011, the povery level for Asian Americans increased by 37%, which surpasses the US national increase of 27% (Ramakrishnan). Another conclusion that come from the Model Minority effect is that Asians are taking over America. While the population of Asian's in America is dramatically increasing, the etimatin on the net effect of immigration is not taking into account different factors. The net effect of immigration status for Asian Americans is "unwarranted for Asian Americans because it is based on studies that mostly compare native-born whites with foreign-born Asian Americans" (Sakamoto). This conclusion does not differentiate a net immigration effect from a new racial effect. (insert more facts?)

Overall, the Model Minority theory is penalizing Asians of a preconceived way to which they must function in life and is encouraging discriminating and racist behavior from outside sources. Many seem to believe that everything about the Asian stereotype is "positive" so it's not really a problem. However, what people seem to forget is the indivuals in the Asian community are not all one. Not every Asian is having the "smart Asian" effect, or derives from a "wealthy, successful" family. By grouping an entire ethnic population into one and assuming they all function the same, puts a strain on the individuals to live up to their expectations. In turn, this also shames those who stand different from the group, such as those who aren't as smart in school, or aren't the typical "quiet nerd". The Model Minority theory is a myth and what is important to attain is that just like every ethnicity, there will be people who are very successful, but there are also those who are still living on the streets trying to make it on their own.

Word Count: 2523

Works Cited

Maddux, William W., et al. "When being a Model Minority is Good . and Bad: Realistic Threat Explains Negativity Toward Asian Americans." Personality and Social Psychology Bulletin, vol. 34, no. 1, 2008, pp. 74-89, doi:10.1177/0146167207309195.

Cheryan, Sapna, and Galen V. Bodenhausen. "When Positive Stereotypes Threaten Intellectual Performance: The Psychological Hazards of "Model Minority" Status." Psychological Science, vol. 11, no. 5, 2000, pp. 399-402, doi:10.1111/1467-9280.00277.

Zhen, Anna. "A Review of the Negative Effects of Seemingly Positive Stereotyping of Asians and Asian Americans on Their Academic Performance and Health." JOURNAL OF PSYCHOLOGY (2016): 23.

Strauss, Valerie. Asian Americans File Complaint Alleging Discrimination in Harvard Admissions. WP Company LLC d/b/a The Washington Post, Washington, 2015.

"Does the 'Bamboo Ceiling' Shut Asian Americans Out of Top Jobs?", National Public Radio, 2014.

Johnson, Stephanie. https://hbr.org/2016/12/why-arent-there-more-asian-americans-in-leadership-positions

Chin, Margaret M. "Asian Americans, Bamboo Ceilings, and Affirmative Action." Contexts, vol. 15, no. 1, 2016, pp. 70-73, doi:10.1177/1536504216628845.

Rhoda J. Yen, "Racial Stereotyping of Asians and Asian Americans and Its Effect on Criminal Justice: A Reflection on the Wayne Lo Case," 7

Asian Am. L.J. 1 (2000). Available at: http://scholarship.law. berkeley.edu/aalj/vol7/iss1/1

Macartney, Suzanne. https://www.census.gov/prod/2013pubs/acsbr11-17.pdf

Sakamoto, Arthur, et al. "The Myth of the Model Minority Myth." Sociological Spectrum, vol. 32, no. 4, 2012, pp. 309-321, doi: 10.1080/02732173.2012.664042.

Ramakrishnan, Karthick, et. Al. https://cdn.americanprogress.org/wp-content/uploads/2014/08/AAPI-IncomePoverty.pdf

ANNA'S FINAL REVISION

The "Wrong Kind" of Asian

I am Asian. Growing up in a Caucasian-populated town, I am an easy target for bullies. I am always the odd one out. My outward appearance does not look like everyone else's. Not everyone accepts my nationality, but I am proud of it. As a young child, I never considered myself "different." My parents are both white. While I was growing up, they have always made me feel like I belonged. My point-of-view was changed when someone pointed out to me that I was different from everyone else. "Your eyes look different than mine" is the statement that started it all and continues to be pointed out to me. I remember going home that night and wondering why my eyes were different from everyone else's. This was something I pondered over for several years. Why was I continuously criticized for something so inconsequential?

The racist jokes I receive are usually all the same: "Open your eyes," "Go back to the rice picking fields," "You have to be smart... You're Asian." The last comment is a stereotype that derives from the "Model Minority" representation of Asian Americans, which perceives the overall Asian American race as socioeconomically successful over all other groups. According to Taylor and Stern, both who are Professors in the US, Asian Americans are considered a "model minority" due to their "affluence, high education, and managerial/professional occupations- and rapid growth in number". The Model Minority theory leaves Asians behind with a preconceived way of how they must function in life and provokes discriminating and racist behavior.

Similar to all other racial stereotypes, Asian Americans are subjected to a variety of stereotypes. Racial slang is often thrown in my face on the daily, yet sometimes I wonder where people are attaining their information from and if they fully understand what they are saying. Several of the Asian stereotypes that are used today correlate with the events that have happened in the past. The Immigration Act of 1965 welcomed large numbers of Asians to enter the United States to work. Before this act, immigration into the US was regulated by the National Origins system, which "limited immigration from Asian to token levels" ("Origins"). The new

Immigration Act abolished restrictive quotas and relaxed the preference system. A new wave of Asians who were previously denied access were now allowed to immigrate to the US. However, it only provided mass entry for those who fit the certain classes required of Asians. The requirement only allowed the wealthiest and educated from each Asian country into the US. After immigrating the certain classes, others who did not fit into these were then recruited to immigrate to the US. The wealthiest/ most educated were drafted first, and then others were recruited. Policymakers sought this plan to fill scientific and technical positions that American students could not successfully fill. As a result, the immigration policy "controlled the quality of Asian immigrants in ways that they did not for other minorities" (Yen 3). Thus, the inundation of successful Asians into America all at one time created a change in character for the Asian community, who were once viewed as aliens and a threat to wage-earners already in the US.

The rise in Asian immigrants created strains between the original American occupants and the newly moved minority group. The American citizens immediately blamed many Asians for assuming control and taking over their communities. Several of the second-generation Asian Americans began working with the successful white Americans, which curated the white Americans ideas of Asian Americans as The Model Minority. The term "model minority" was first introduced in January 1966 in a *New York Times Magazine* by sociologist William Petersen. In his article, "Success Story: Japanese American Style," the success of Japanese Americans is emphasized upon because the Japanese were thought to be the closest related to Americans; thus, several people "quickly generalized across all Asian ethnic groups, regardless of their diversity in culture, education, and class" (Yoo). The success of newly immigrated Asians appeared in numerous press articles. However, the Immigration Act of 1965 was often overlooked in Petersen's coining of "model minority." The lifting of restrictions and recruiting of professionals is what ultimately created the large influx of successful Asian Americans. Petersen's term also concealed the discrepancies of other concepts, such as income, education, and health. The model minority term has led to the stereotyping of Asians that is now affecting current generations.

The Model Minority stereotype is proof that some racial stereotypes can seem favorable. However, the people of the group can also be exploited in a negative way. The model-minority image brings about several problems. One of the major implications that arise is harsh stereotyping and discrimination. The Model Minority theory has created several stereotypes that create a generalization across all Asian Americans, despite the multiple different backgrounds that they come from. Although much of the stereotyping of Asians are positive and can seem like a compliment to those outside of the ethnicity, much of the assumptions can be harmful. Considering all Asians as "successful" and "hardworking" does not bring to truth the factors that ultimately leaves the Asian community at disadvantage by lumping the entire ethnic group into one stereotype. A study was conducted that focused on Asian-American participants' ethnicity and was hypothesized to make them derive better test scores than those participants whose identities were not acknowledged beforehand. The study predicted that by making the ethnicity salient before taking the test, there would be an enhanced test score from Asians in particular. However, the study resulted in, "under these conditions, ethnicity salience resulted in diminished ability to concentrate, which in turn led to significantly impaired math performance" (Cheryan and Bodenhausen 1). This research is crucial considering that people hold positive stereotypes over Asians and their mathematical skills. By doing so, this creates high pressure for the Asian community and can result in a negative performance on a test, which may affect the future for the new generation.

Additionally, the Model Minority theory forces upon the idea that Asians are not outstanding communicators due to the language barrier and are therefore quiet and silent. However, this is affecting several Asian Americans and Pacific Islander students in the classroom as this stereotypical image "may also pose pressure upon them to violate their cultural upbringing and conform to the Western norms in the classroom, where grades are often based upon students' verbal participation" (Kwon et al. 10). In result of conforming, this can conflictingly affect the relationship between parent and child of Asian ethnicity. Several Asian families come with their ethics and morals. The Model Minority theory can put pressure on young Asian students to change their ways in the classroom from what they were previously raised to do.

The Asian stereotypes that are driven from the Model Minority Theory are often ignored because several people outside of the

Asian ethnicity view the image as something "positive." The typical "smart Asian" stereotype leads everyone to conclude that if you're Asian, you must be smart. In turn, this puts a lot of pressure on Asians who are not "naturally smart" to attempt to live up to their standard or else face outside judgment. Many Asians feel that they are unable to create an image for themselves, but rather already have a template waiting for them to fill. The pressure to fill this template is discussed in *Asian American Law Journal*. Daya Sandhu, a Professor of Educational and Counseling Psychology, explained that the social pressure to fulfill the "smart Asian" stereotype causes numerous "mental health concerns and psychological afflictions, such as threats to cultural identity, powerlessness, feelings of marginality, loneliness, hostility and perceived alienation and discrimination" (qtd. in Yen 6). Since the stereotype is prevalent to much of society, Asians often take the racism that is handed to them. Current research by William Maddux, a professor at INSEAD, tried to explain the reasoning for the stereotyping. The research demonstrates that the Asian American perception created by the Model Minority theory creates a sense of threat and competition to other groups regarding economic-wise, which in turn may lead to the negative attitudes and emotions towards the Asians (Maddux et al. 1). This reasoning demonstrates that people are unaware of the diverse ethnic identity and background that appears within the Asian American group, and therefore make assumptions from an outdated myth.

In addition to receiving racial hinders, Asian Americans are also affected by the Model Minority in institutional organizations such as the workplace and college. Although a majority of the Asian community has differing levels of college degrees, many are only being used for low-level jobs. An Asian American organization, ASCEND, collected data from HP, Intel, Google, LinkedIn, and Yahoo to show that within these top companies, "Asian Americans represent 27% of professionals, 19% of managers, and just 14% of executives" (Chin). It was additionally calculated that "in these five firms, white men and women are 154% more likely than Asians to hold an executive role" (Johnson and Sy 1). The Model Minority represents Asians as a group of hardworking individuals who thrive to be successful and pass the work-ethic drive onto their offspring. The naturally "smart Asian" stereotype mentioned above, tends to follow Asians throughout their life, even in the professional field. So why aren't Asians advancing in the workplace? Jane Hyun explained the situation by coining the term "Bamboo Ceiling," similar to the "Glass Ceiling" effect (Chen). This term examines the level of diversity while climbing the corporate ladder. It can be seen in any business; the higher you climb, the less diversity is found. This can revert to the stereotyping of Asians as poor communicators, which is a big turn off for a leadership position.

Another reason why Asian Americans may not be reaching the leadership spots in the professional workplace is due to college admissions. Much of the Asian population attends Ivy-League schools and elite universities nationwide and are continuing to overtake fields such as medicine, engineering, and computer science. However, their representation at Harvard University is solidly stable, with no increase or decrease. With the increase in the population of Asian Americans rising sharply, there is much speculation for why Harvard's count for Asian Americans isn't increasing. It is believed that Harvard has a quota in which they limit their Asian American representation and therefore reject several Asian students despite their top-notch performances. According to Valerie Strauss, a Washington DC reporter, "many Asian-American students who have almost perfect SAT scores, top 1% GPAs, plus significant awards or leadership positions in various extracurricular activities have been rejected by Harvard University" (Strauss). In response, the Asian community filed a complaint against Harvard complaining that they are using racial quotas to admit students other than the Asians. While this is a severe problem, many Asian Americans are choosing to opt around this roadblock to their college admission. Brian Taylor, an Ivy League coach out of Manhattan, is directing his clients not to check "Asian" when applying for colleges as this makes the student appear "less Asian" and therefore appear as just a "normal" smart student (English). This is creating a strain on Asian students as they have their future to worry for due to their ethnicity.

Despite the Model Minority theory that has created the strong stereotypes of Asians, this model seems to be more of a myth than something to follow. The Model Minority isolates the Asian population in a way that can tragically hurt them. It creates high expectations that can be proven wrong. The Model Minority myth presents Asians as successful in their careers with a financially stable background. When examining the poverty rates in 2007-2011 published by the US Census, Asian Americans ranked one of the lowest poverty rates according to race at 12.8%., with whites ranking comparable (Macartney et al. 1). However, when looking closer at the data, Asian Americans were experiencing the fastest growth in poverty rates in the United States. According to the Center for American Progress, during the same term of 2007-2011, the poverty level for Asian Americans increased by 37%, which surpasses the US national increase of 27% (Ramakrishnan and Ahmad). Another conclusion that comes from the Model Minority effect is that Asians are taking over America. While the population of Asians in America is dramatically increasing, the estimation of the net effect of immigration is not taking into account the different factors. The net effect of immigration status for Asian Americans is being mistaken as "the difference in means between a group of immigrants and a group of non-immigrants who are otherwise similar" (Sakamoto et al. 312). This conclusion does not differentiate a net immigration effect from a new racial effect. The Asian stereotype is created by dismissing various aspects and jumping straight to conclusions.

Overall, the Model Minority theory is penalizing Asians of a preconceived way to which they must function in life and is encouraging discriminating and racist behavior from outside sources. However, the Model Minority theory is negatively affecting the Asian American population in the US, rather than helping them. The racist stereotyping that is derived from the theory is leading to poor performance on tests due to the high pressure the stereotype holds upon Asians. Additionally, the Model Minority theory is affecting Asian Americans' ability to get into Ivy League schools and move up corporate ladders in their careers. Given my Asian ethnicity, I have yet to experience any negative effects of the Model Minority stereotype. However, this still directly affects me as I head into my future knowing that I may be at an unfair advantage due the color of my face and the shape of my eyes. Looking forward, I hope to see a future with no stereotypes based on the Model Minority theory as this is simply a myth that has evolved into a generalization of an entire ethnic population.

Word Count: 2308

Works Cited

Chen, Liyan. "How Asian Americans Can Break Through the Bamboo Ceiling." *Forbes,* 20 Jan. 2016, www.forbes.com/sites/liyanchen/2016/01/20/how-asian-americans-can-break-through-the-bamboo-ceiling/#1791cc0b1e43

Cheryan, Sapna, and Galen V. Bodenhausen. "When Positive Stereotypes Threaten Intellectual Performance: The Psychological Hazards of 'Model Minority' Status." *Psychological Science*, vol. 11, no. 5, Sep. 2000, pp 399-402, *Sage Journals*, doi:10.1111/1467-9280.00277.

Chin, Margaret M. "Asian Americans, Bamboo Ceilings, and Affirmative Action." Contexts, vol. 15, no. 1, 2016, pp. 70-73, *Sage Journals,* doi:10.1177/1536504216628845.

English, Bella. "To get into Elite Colleges, Some Advised to 'Appear Less Asian'." *Boston Globe*, Boston Glove Media Partners, LLC, 01 June 2015, www.bostonglobe.com/lifestyle/2015/06/01/college-counselors-advise-some-asian-students-appear-less-asian/Ew7g4JiQMiqYNQlIwqEIuO/story.html

Johnson, Stephanie, and Thomas Sy. "Why Aren't There More Asian Americans in Leadership Positions?" *Harvard Business Review*, Harvard Business Publishing, 19 Dec. 2016, hbr.org/2016/12/why-arent-there-more-asian-americans-in-leadership-positions

Kwon, Jimin, et al. "Stereotype Threat on Asian American College Students." *Advanced Science and Technology Letters*, vol. 59, 2014, pp. 7-13, dx.doi.org/10.14257/astl.2014.59.02

Macartney, Suzanne, et. al. "Poverty Rates for Selected Detailed Race and Hispanic Groups by State and Place: 2007-2011." US Census Bureau, American Community Survey, 2007-2011. Feb. 2013. www.census.gov/prod/2013pubs/acsbr11-17.pdf

Maddux, William W., et al. "When being a Model Minority is Good… and Bad: Realistic Threat Explains Negativity Toward Asian Americans." *Personality and Social Psychology Bulletin*, vol. 34, no. 1, Sage Publications, 2008, pp. 74-89, *Sage Journals* doi:10.1177/0146167207309195.

"Origins of the 1965 Immigration Act." *The 1965 Immigration Act: Asian-Nation*, www.asian-nation.org/1965-immigration-act.shtml.

Ramakrishnan, Karthick, and Farah Z. Ahmad. "Income and Poverty: Part of the 'State of Asian Americans and Pacific Islanders' Series." *Center for American Progress*, 21 July 2014. cdn.americanprogress.org/wp-content/uploads/2014/08/AAPI-IncomePoverty.pdf

Sakamoto, Arthur, et al. "The Myth of the Model Minority Myth." *Sociological Spectrum*, vol. 32, no. 4, Taylor and Francis Group2012, pp. 309-321, *EBSCOhost*, doi:10.1080/02732173.2012.664042.

Strauss, Valerie. "Asian Americans File Complaint Alleging Discrimination in Harvard Admissions." *The Washington Post*, 16 May 2015, www.washingtonpost.com/news/answer-sheet/wp/2015/05/16/asian-americans-file-complaint-alleging-discrimination-in-harvard-admissions/?utm_term=.dc64d3780dbf

Taylor, Charles R., and Barbara B. Stern. "Asian-Americans: Television Advertising and the 'Model Minority' Stereotype." *Journal of Advertising*, vol. 26, no. 2, Taylor and Francis Ltd, 1997, *Michigan Library*, www.jstor.org/stable/4189033

Yen, Rhoda J. "Racial Stereotyping of Asians and Asian Americans and Its Effect on Criminal Justice: A Reflection on the Wayne Lo Case," *Asian American Law Journal*, vol. 7, no. 1, pp. 1-28, scholarship.law.berkeley.edu/aalj/vol7/iss1/1

Yoo, Brandon. "Unraveling the Model Minority Myth of Asian American Students." *Education.com*, 25 Oct. 2010, www.education.com/reference/article/unraveling-minority-myth-asian-students/.

UNIVERSITY AND WRITING DEPARTMENT POLICIES

WRT 150 sections can have many differences in terms of assignments, daily routines, and instruction. We want all instructors to teach in the ways that best suit their abilities and the needs of their particular students. Nevertheless, as part of our effort to ensure consistency across sections, all WRT 150 instructors adhere to the following university and departmental policies.

REQUIRED PASSING GRADE

You must pass WRT 150 with a grade of C or better (above C–) to satisfy Grand Valley's Writing Foundation Requirement. If you do not receive a grade of C or better, you will need to take WRT 150 again.

LEARNING OR PHYSICAL DISABILITIES

If you have any special needs because of learning, physical, or any other disabilities, please contact Disability Support Resources at 616-331-2490. Any student needing academic accommodations beyond those given to the entire class needs to request assistance from DSR. Writing faculty work with DSR to accommodate students' special needs and devise a plan that is fair to all students. Furthermore, if you have a disability and think you will need assistance evacuating a classroom and/or building in an emergency situation, please make your instructor and DSR aware so that Grand Valley can develop a plan to assist you.

ATTENDANCE

Regular, timely, and full attendance is required to succeed in WRT 150. According to the Grand Valley catalog, instructors may fail students for excessive absences. In WRT 150, missing class more than four times constitutes excessive absences, and can be grounds for failing the course. Tardiness, leaving class while it is in session, coming unprepared, or off-task behavior (like texting) may also count as an absence or partial absence according to your instructor's policies. You might receive an e-mail warning from your instructor after the fourth absence, but it is your responsibility to keep track of your attendance. Excessive absence itself is the grounds for failure, so that lack of warning does not excuse any further absences. The warning simply provides additional clarity.

THE WRT 150 PORTFOLIO

Many professionals use portfolios to show other people what they are capable of producing. Your WRT 150 portfolio represents your own end-of-semester writing capabilities. The portfolio includes three fully revised and polished papers, including at least one that integrates outside sources and accurately credits the ideas and language drawn from those sources. Together, these three pieces of writing produce your final letter grade.

The three papers in your portfolio represent your abilities as a college-level academic writer, so you should select and revise them with care. For example, you probably do not want three very short papers, since that would fail to show your ability to write a longer paper. Ask your instructor and peer reviewers about your selections if you are not sure. Your instructor and the other students should help you make good choices about what goes in the final portfolio. Also, read the full portfolios published in this book, and, together with your instructor and classmates, try to learn from them what makes a WRT 150 portfolio successful.

So that your instructor has time to check all work for any problems, we strictly enforce your instructor's requirements for turning in earlier versions of work that you intend to place in your portfolio. All papers in your portfolio must have been assigned for the class and seen by your instructor in draft form before final submission.

CHARACTERISTICS OF A, B, C, AND D PORTFOLIOS

We provide the general characteristics of A, B, and C portfolios for you here so that you can identify precisely how your work is evaluated. Characteristics that cause portfolios to fall below the standard for a passing grade are presented as characteristics of D papers. Factors that can cause you to receive an F for the course are listed at the end of the grading criteria. Your instructor, with the help of the instructor's portfolio grading group, will develop more specific understandings of these criteria to apply to your exact assignments and portfolios; in doing so, however, all of them will be seeking to apply the general characteristics accurately and fairly to your work.

Characteristics of A Portfolios

Content and Research

▶ The portfolio consistently engages the interest of intelligent and sophisticated college-level readers.

▶ Papers effectively address and engage their likely and intended audiences.

▶ Papers succeed at accomplishing challenging purposes.

▶ Each paper maintains a consistent focus on the main claim or goal for the paper.

▶ Each paper develops its focus with significant and interesting discussion, details, and examples, including graphics when useful.

▶ The portfolio clearly demonstrates the writer's information literacy and ability to use college-level academic research as a significant means to develop the writer's complex ideas.

▶ The portfolio clearly demonstrates the writer's ability to introduce and integrate material from relevant outside sources to advance the purposes for the writing and meet the expectations of intelligent and sophisticated college-level readers.

Organization

▶ Titles and opening sections of papers inform readers appropriately of the topic, purpose, and focus of the paper in ways that motivate readers to continue reading.

▶ Paragraphs are purposefully organized and substantially developed with supporting evidence, examples, and reasoning.

▶ Paragraphs break information into parts that contribute to a greater understanding of the whole.

▶ Readers can easily see how the order in which information appears supports the focus and purpose of the papers.

▶ The papers lead readers through the order of the discussion in ways that are explicit, clear, and purposeful, including effective transition devices when needed.

▶ Readers can see a meaningful pattern in the order of the information as a whole.

▶ Closing sections give readers a satisfied sense that the purpose of the writing has been achieved.

Style

▶ Word choice is precise, interesting, and appropriate to the writing purpose and audience.

▶ Language is mature and purposefully controlled.

▶ Sentences are clear, logical, enjoyable, and easily understood by college-level readers.

▶ Sentences often make active statements and use efficient and effective modification.

▶ Sentence structure varies according to the content, purpose, and audience.

▶ A consistent voice complements each paper's purpose, fits its genre, and appeals to its likely and intended readers.

▶ Information and quotations from sources are integrated skillfully into the writer's own sentences and paragraphs.

Mechanics

▶ Format is consistent with the detailed requirements of an applicable style guide, such as the MLA or APA style guides.

▶ References to outside sources are cited and documented according to the appropriate style guide carefully enough that readers can easily identify the sources that have been quoted or referenced.

▶ Problems in grammar, spelling, punctuation, or usage do not interfere with communication.

▶ Editing shows effective attention to the desire of readers to read without being interrupted by unexpected errors or problems with documentation and format.

Characteristics of B Portfolios

Content and Research

- The portfolio connects with the interest of intelligent and sophisticated college-level readers.
- Papers clearly address the expectations of their likely and intended audiences.
- Papers accomplish or make strong attempts to accomplish challenging purposes.
- Each paper maintains a consistent, single focus.
- Each paper develops a focus with fitting and relevant discussions, details, and examples, including graphics when useful.
- The portfolio demonstrates the writer's ability to use college-level academic research clearly and purposefully to develop the writer's ideas.
- The portfolio demonstrates the writer's ability to introduce and integrate material from relevant outside sources in ways that enhance the accomplishment of goals and purposes.

Organization

- Titles and opening sections of papers are well-chosen and appropriate to the topic and focus of the papers.
- Paragraphs are clearly organized and adequately developed with supporting evidence, examples, and reasoning, though some paragraphs may lack richness of detail or evidence.
- Paragraphs break information into parts that make sense and assist effective reading.
- Readers can identify the focus of each paper and follow it through the entire discussion.
- Readers can identify how the order in which information appears supports the focus and purpose of the papers.
- Overall patterns in the order of presentation make sense.
- Transitions between and within paragraphs advance the writer's ideas.
- Closing sections give readers a clear sense that the writer is ending the discussion at a good place.

Style

- Word choice is generally appropriate to the writing purpose and audience.
- Language is generally mature and purposefully controlled.
- Sentences are generally clear, logical, and readable.
- Sentences typically make active statements, extended by efficient and effective modification.
- Sentences vary in structure and only occasionally are choppy, rambling, or repetitive.
- The voice in each paper is consistent and appropriate for the writer's genre, purpose, and audience.
- Information and quotations from sources make sense within the writer's own sentences and paragraphs.

Mechanics

- Format is appropriate and generally follows the requirements of an assigned style guide, such as MLA or APA.
- References to outside sources are cited and documented according to the appropriate style guide carefully enough that readers can determine when source material has been used and find the sources.
- Mistakes in grammar, spelling, punctuation, or usage rarely interfere with communication.
- Editing shows attention to the desire of readers to read without being interrupted by unexpected errors.

Characteristics of C Portfolios

Content and Research

► The portfolio makes sense to intelligent and sophisticated college-level readers, though it may not consistently hold their interest.

► The portfolio presents ideas and descriptions with readers in mind.

► Papers appear to aim at accomplishing purposes.

► Each paper generally maintains a single focus, though the focus may be on a topic or an event rather than an idea, claim, or goal.

► Each paper generally develops a focus with details, examples, and discussions, including graphics when useful.

► The portfolio demonstrates the writer's ability to use relevant college-level academic research as a means to discuss a topic.

► The portfolio demonstrates the writer's ability to include material from outside sources within the general requirements of an applicable style guide.

Organization

► Titles and openings generally match the topic and focus.

► Paragraphs make sense and usually use some evidence or detailed examples to support points.

► Papers generally establish an overall organizational pattern for readers to follow.

► Each paper develops a basic focus, with few paragraphs appearing to be out of sequence or off-track.

► Transitions from one section and idea to another are evident and make sense.

Style

► Most words appear to be well chosen and fit the purpose and audience for the particular paper.

► Some of the sentences are short and choppy, long and rambling, vague and wordy, or repetitive.

► Sentences are generally readable and make sense.

► Sentences sometimes feature the efficient and effective uses of modifying clauses and phrases.

► The writer's voice is usually consistent and appropriate, fitting the writer's genre, purpose, and audience.

► Information and quoted language from sources is clearly presented as source material.

Mechanics

► Format choices are generally appropriate for the purposes of the papers.

► References to outside sources are generally cited and documented, if not always in the appropriate style; readers can determine when source material has been quoted or referenced, and instances of unreferenced source material are few and clearly not intentional.

► Mistakes in grammar, spelling, punctuation, or usage do not generally interfere with either the writer's credibility or the reader's ability to read the text easily.

► Editing shows adequate attention to the desire of readers to read without being interrupted by unexpected errors.

Characteristics of D Portfolios

Content and Research

- Topics, purposes, claims, or focuses are so simplistic and obvious that they do not engage the interest of college-educated readers.
- Papers have no apparent and appropriate audiences.
- Papers have no clear purposes.
- At least one paper is clearly fictional.
- Papers lack a single focus.
- Ideas are stated, but they are not developed with details, examples, and discussions.
- Language and material from sources are consistently presented in ways that are very hard to follow.
- Unintentional, careless misuse of source material would amount to plagiarism had it been intentional.
- The portfolio shows weak research and information literacy skills, such as the use of very few sources, little variety of sources, or little obvious effort to conduct scholarly or professional research.
- Sources do not support and may even contradict the views that the writer attributes to them.

Organization

- Openings and endings are missing, misleading, or overly general.
- Readers cannot readily see the focus of the papers.
- Paragraphs frequently seem unrelated to each other or repetitive.
- Paragraphs do not develop logically from start to finish, or they break in illogical places.
- Paragraphs often end without developing broad, general statements with evidence and reasoning.
- Transitions between and within paragraphs are weak, ineffective, or misleading.
- The papers do not establish clear patterns for readers to follow.

Style

- Sentences are often short and choppy, long and rambling, vague and wordy, or repetitive.
- Disordered sentence parts, poor phrasing, and poor word choices make reading difficult.
- Sentences often disregard the normal rules of standard written English in ways that make ideas hard to understand.
- The voice often appears inappropriate for the writer's purpose, genre, and audience.

Mechanics

- Format, including any use of graphics, is extremely careless or entirely disregards the basic requirements of applicable style guides.
- Language or material from outside sources is not clearly cited.
- Documentation style is generally wrong according to the assigned style guide, often in ways that interfere with readers' abilities to find the source material and locate the referenced portions of the sources.
- Instances of misused source material show careless inattention to important requirements for quoting, paraphrasing, and citing, raising questions of possible plagiarism.
- Many errors in spelling, grammar, punctuation, word choice, and usage make reading difficult, or they strongly limit the writer's credibility.

Regardless of overall student writing ability, portfolios will receive the grade of D if, as a whole, the portfolio fails to demonstrate that the student understands how to conduct college-level research as well as how to integrate the results of his/her research into purposeful writing without committing plagiarism. Otherwise, D portfolios rarely have similar characteristics. The lists below present the characteristics that help predict when a portfolio does not demonstrate competence. **The main key to avoiding a D is to meet the criteria for at least a C.**

F Grades

The grade of F in WRT 150 is reserved for the following circumstances:

> ▸ The student did not turn in a portfolio by the last day of class (or the due date set by the instructor's syllabus, if the instructor chooses another due date).

> ▸ The portfolio did not have three papers in it that qualified for the portfolio under this Guide and the instructor's syllabus.

> ▸ The student violated course polices set by this Guide or the instructor's syllabus (for example, an attendance policy), if the information made clear that the violation would result in a grade of F.

> ▸ The student violated other policies of Grand Valley State University that clearly state that the violation could result in a grade of F.

> ▸ The student clearly committed plagiarism, as described by Grand Valley's Student Code, this Guide, and the instructor's syllabus.

> ▸ The portfolio clearly demonstrates a complete indifference to earning any higher grade.

On the next few pages, you'll see the same portfolio characteristics you just read presented another way. This chart allows you to compare the differences for each grade level for the different criteria we will look at when we evaluate your drafts and final essays.

CONTENT AND RESEARCH

A Paper Characteristics	B Paper Characteristics	C Paper Characteristics	D Paper Characteristics
Content: consistently engages interest of intelligent, sophisticated college-level readers (intended audience); accomplishes challenging purposes.	**Content:** connects with intelligent, sophisticated college-level readers; clearly addresses audience's expectations; accomplishes or makes strong attempt to accomplish challenging purposes.	**Content:** makes sense to intelligent, sophisticated college-level readers, though may not hold interest consistently; presents ideas and descriptions with audience in mind; appears to aim at accomplishing a purpose.	**Content:** topics, purposes, claims, or focus are so simple and obvious that they fail to engage interest of college-level reader; no apparent and appropriate audience; no clear purpose; at least one paper in portfolio is clearly fictional.
Focus: maintained on main claim/goal; developed with significant, interesting discussion, details, and examples (including graphics when useful).	**Focus:** consistent and single focus; developed with fitting/relevant discussions, details, and examples (including graphics when useful).	**Focus:** maintains single focus, though might be on a topic/event rather than an idea, claim, or goal; generally develops focus with details, examples, and discussions (including graphics when useful).	**Focus:** lacks single focus; ideas are stated but not developed with details, examples, and discussions.
Information Literacy: demonstrates ability to use college-level academic research to develop complex ideas significantly.	**Information Literacy:** demonstrates ability to use college-level academic research to develop ideas.	**Information Literacy:** demonstrates ability to use relevant college-level academic research to discuss topic.	**Information Literacy:** weak research and information literacy ability: very few sources, little variety of sources, and little obvious effort to conduct scholarly/professional research.
Sources: introduced and integrated to advance essay's purpose and meet audience expectations.	**Sources:** introduced and integrated in ways that meet the essay's goals and purposes.	**Sources:** included within the general requirements of an applicable style guide.	**Sources:** language and materials from sources presented is hard-to-follow; unintentional, careless misuse of source material would be plagiarism if intentional; sources do not support and might contradict writer's views attributed to them.

ORGANIZATION

A Paper Characteristics	B Paper Characteristics	C Paper Characteristics	D Paper Characteristics
Title and Introduction: appropriately informs reader of topic, purpose, and focus; motivates audience to read.	**Title and Introduction:** well-chosen, appropriate to topic and focus.	**Title and Introduction:** generally match topic and focus.	**Title and Introduction:** missing, misleading, or overly general.
Paragraphs: organized purposefully and developed substantially with evidence, examples, and reasoning.	**Paragraphs:** organized clearly and developed adequately with evidence, examples, and reasoning; some paragraphs may lack richness of detail or evidence.	**Paragraphs:** make sense, points usually supported with some evidence or detailed examples.	**Paragraphs:** frequently unrelated to each other or repetitive; don't develop logically from start to finish, or break in illogical places; often end without developing broad, general statements with evidence and reasoning.
Paragraphing: contributes to greater understanding of the whole.	**Paragraphing:** information broken into parts that make sense, assist effective reading.	**Paragraphing:** generally establishes overall organizational pattern for readers to follow.	**Paragraphing:** shows a weak organization pattern; can be difficult to understand how one paragraph is connected to the next.
Order of Discussion: paper guides reader in explicit, clear, and purposeful ways (including transitions when necessary).	**Order of Discussion:** focus is identifiable and can be followed through entire discussion; transitions between and within paragraphs advance writer's ideas.	**Order of Discussion:** develops basic focus, with few paragraphs out of sequence or off track; transitions from one section/idea to another are evident and make sense.	**Order of Discussion:** focus is not readily apparent; transitions between and within paragraphs are weak, ineffective, or misleading.
Order of Information: ordered in a meaningful pattern; order of information clearly supports focus and purpose.	**Order of Information:** focus and purpose are identifiable by order in which information appears; overall patterns make sense.	**Order of Information:** some patterns make sense, though the overall focus may be unclear.	**Order of Information:** does not establish clear patterns for readers to follow.
Conclusion: satisfying sense that purpose has been achieved.	**Conclusion:** gives sense that the discussion ends at a good place.	**Conclusion:** may summarize the ideas in the essay but does not explain why ideas are significant.	**Conclusion:** essay ends abruptly and without resolution.

STYLE

A Paper Characteristics	B Paper Characteristics	C Paper Characteristics	D Paper Characteristics
Word choice: precise, interesting, appropriate to writing purpose and audience.	**Word choice:** generally appropriate to writing purpose and audience.	**Word choice:** most words well-chosen and fit purpose and audience.	**Word choice:** poor word choices make reading difficult.
Language: mature, purposefully controlled.	**Language:** generally mature and purposefully controlled.	**Language:** somewhat mature and controlled.	**Language:** uncontrolled use of language; simplistic vocabulary throughout.
Sentences: often active statements; uses efficient and effective modification.	**Sentences:** typically active statements, extended by efficient and effective modification.	**Sentences:** generally readable and make sense; sometimes feature efficient and effective modifying clauses/phrases.	**Sentences:** disordered sentence parts, poor phrasing; make reading difficult; often disregard normal rules of standard written English in ways that make ideas hard to understand.
Sentence Structure: varies according to content, purpose, and audience.	**Sentence Structure:** varies in structure, only occasionally is choppy, rambling, or repetitive.	**Sentence Structure:** sentences are occasionally choppy, long and rambling, vague and wordy ,or repetitive.	**Sentence Structure:** often short and choppy, long and rambling, vague and wordy, or repetitive.
Voice: consistent, complements purpose, fits the genre, and appeals to audience.	**Voice:** consistent and appropriate for genre, purpose, and audience.	**Voice:** consistent and appropriate, usually fitting genre, purpose, and audience.	**Voice:** often inappropriate for genre, purpose, and audience.
Sources: information and quotes integrated skillfully into writer's own sentences and paragraphs.	**Sources:** information and quotes make sense within writer's own sentences and paragraphs.	**Sources:** information and quotes clearly presented as source material.	**Sources:** information and quotes dropped into paragraphs without context or transitions.

MECHANICS

A Paper Characteristics	B Paper Characteristics	C Paper Characteristics	D Paper Characteristics
Format: consistent with MLA, APA, or other style guide.	**Format:** appropriate, generally follows MLA, APA, or other style guide.	**Format:** generally appropriate for the purpose, usually floows MLA, APA, or other style guide.	**Format:** careless attention to basic requirements of applicable style guides (including use of graphics).
References: cited and documented according to appropriate style guide so quoted sources are easily identified.	**References:** cited and documented according to appropriate style guide so it can be determined when sources have been used and can be found.	**References:** generally cited and documented, if not always appropriately; reader can determine when sources are quoted or referenced; instances of unreferenced sources are few and clearly not intentional.	**References:** language or material not cited clearly; documentation is generally wrong according to assigned style guide, often in ways that interfere with reader's ability to find source material and locate referenced portions; shows careless attention to important requirements for quoting, paraphrasing, and citing, raising questions of possible plagiarism.
Grammar, Spelling, Punctuation: do not interfere with communication.	**Grammar, Spelling, Punctuation:** mistakes rarely interfere with communication.	**Grammar, Spelling, Punctuation:** mistakes sometimes interfere with writer's credibility or reader's ability to read easily.	**Grammar, Spelling, Punctuation:** many errors in spelling, grammar, punctuation, word choice, and usage make reading difficult or limit writer's credibility.
Editing: effectively shows attention to audience's desire to read without interruption from unexpected errors.	**Editing:** usually shows attention to audience's desire to read without interruption from unexpected errors.	**Editing:** shows some attention to reader's desire to read without interruption from unexpected errors.	**Editing:** does not show attention to reader's desire to read without interruption from unexpected errors.

GRADING IN WRT 150

PORTFOLIO SUBMISSION GUIDELINES

Your portfolio is due by the end of the last class before finals week, unless your instructor's syllabus sets a different deadline. Electronic portfolios will be prepared and submitted according to instructions that you will receive in class and that are found on the WRT 150 portfolio site (https://www.gvsu.edu/writing/portfolio). If your portfolio is late, you may fail the course.

Your final portfolio will consist of three final papers. The following instructions apply unless your instructor gives you other special instructions:

▶ Margins should be one inch all the way around the page.
▶ All lines should be double-spaced.
▶ Fonts should be common or default types (e.g., Arial, Calibri, Times New Roman), and the point-size should be 11 or 12.

If your instructor has special instructions for the form or format of your papers, the portfolio grading groups will honor those instructions.

In addition to requiring you to submit earlier drafts, your instructor is entitled to set further requirements before your portfolio will be eligible for grading. Common requirements are that you submit papers on time in response to individual assignments, submit substantial revisions, use particular formats, or submit papers at a specific length or level of editing care. If you do not meet your instructor's specific requirements, your instructor may refuse to submit your portfolio for grading, in which case you will fail the course. Such requirements will be set out clearly in your instructor's syllabus, assignments, or other written instructions, and if you have questions about those requirements, you should ask your instructor.

Instructors do not comment on portfolios, so your portfolio will not be returned to you. You should keep copies of your work and wait for grade reports to see your course grades. The Department of Writing may keep your portfolio and use it for studies of our teaching and its results, but we will not publish the contents of your writing or share it with future classes without your permission.

PORTFOLIO GRADING

We determine all final grades in WRT 150 by having a group of instructors read and evaluate your final portfolio. Your instructor has been placed in a portfolio group this semester, and this group will grade your portfolio. We use this method so that our grading can be as fair and accurate as possible. Our instructors work very hard to make sure that this method gives you the fairest result.

Over the course of the semester your instructor's portfolio grading group (usually four to six instructors) reads and discusses samples of writing from their classes throughout the semester to agree about standards for A, B, C, and D papers. Their standards begin with those established by the Department of Writing and set forth more specifically earlier in this Guide. Through their discussions, the groups work to fit those standards more specifically to your assignments and the work done by your class.

At the end of the semester, your instructor and one other instructor from the portfolio grading group will read and grade your portfolio. If they disagree about the grade, a third instructor in that group reads your portfolio to decide which reader, your instructor or the other instructor, has come closest to the standards that the portfolio group has agreed upon during the semester. Agreement between two or more instructors determines your letter grade in the class. For example, if your portfolio receives a B from the first two readers, you receive a B on your portfolio. If your portfolio receives an A from one reader, a B from another, and an A from a third reader, you receive an A on your portfolio. By using this method, we seek to arrive at a "community" grade based on the quality of your writing rather than a grade based solely on one instructor's preferences or on your instructor's personal opinion of you.

Once the portfolio grading group arrives at a letter grade, your instructor also has the option of adding a "plus" or "minus" to the final letter grade based on other aspects of your work, such as attendance, class participation, effective peer review, and completion of reading assignments. Instructors should not raise or lower your grade any further than a plus or minus, which ensures the highest degree of fairness based on the quality of your work.

The portfolios are graded after class is over, so the portfolios are not returned. For those reasons, we do not write comments on the papers in the portfolios. Instructors do often write very brief notes about grades of D, so students earning this grade may ask about the reasons for that grade.

If you have any questions about the grade that you receive, ask your instructor to discuss your grade with you.

SEMESTER-LONG EVALUATION

The fact that you earn your grade with your final portfolio does not mean that the evaluation of your writing should be a mystery. First, you should learn how to apply the grading criteria to your own writing. Your instructor will read your writing throughout the semester and respond to it with comments and suggestions for revision. Many instructors will have you read, comment on, and evaluate other students' work. For most students, a grade is not necessary for early drafts because the proper focus is on what the paper could become, not on what it is. But if you want a grade on an assignment and your instructor has not given one, just ask. Instructors will be able to tell you where they think the paper falls within the range of A to D. Your instructor will probably tell you what the portfolio group has been saying about writing like yours.

Nevertheless, it is important to remember that all grade estimates—whether they are by you, your instructor, or your classmates—are just that: estimates. Ultimately, the grade will depend

> *"Take this course seriously. When papers are assigned to you, start right away. Use all the help you can get to make your papers the best."*
> *—Jacob R.*

on the entire portfolio in its final form, something nobody will be able to review carefully until the end of the term. Mainly what you need to do is just keep on working. If the instructor says your paper is probably a low B or a C, your next question should be: "What could I work on in this paper that would improve it?" Improve your work until the very last day, and you will receive the best grade available to you. Meanwhile, you should also seek to improve your own judgment of your own grade, using the grading criteria. The most successful and satisfied WRT 150 students do not need the instructor to tell them what grade they are getting; they already have a good idea themselves.

MIDTERM EVALUATION

Grand Valley requires midterm grade reports for first-year students and some upper-level students. Midterm grades are available on the Web but not recorded on your official transcript. Midterm grades in WRT 150 can only assess the overall quality of your work in the class up to that point and your prospects for doing better. Such assessments have no direct bearing on your final grade. For a full explanation of your midterm grade, please consult with your instructor.

GRADE APPEALS

If for any reason you need to appeal your final grade, please consult the Student Code for the applicable procedures. Your first contact should be with the instructor of your class. Appeals from your instructor's decision to the Department of Writing should be supported by a written appeal explaining how your portfolio displays the characteristics of the grade that you are seeking. Your written appeal itself should display most characteristics of the grade that you seek. Appeals to the Director of First-Year Writing may be forwarded by e-mail at wrtdept@gvsu.edu or delivered to the Department of Writing directed to the attention of the Director of First-Year Writing.

PORTFOLIO GRADING FAQ: QUESTIONS YOU MIGHT HAVE

1. **Why is a group of Writing 150 instructors reading my papers and determining my final grade rather than just my own instructor?**

A group of four to six instructors (including your instructor) has been reading samples of your class's writing throughout the semester to discuss and agree about what is an A, B, C, D, and F paper. The goal of the instructors in the group is to set fair and accurate grading standards. The standards will develop after discussing samples from your class and other classes throughout the semester. This carefully considered agreement between two writing instructors results in more consistent and fair grades than any other method.

2. **Does my instructor have any say as to what grade I get on my portfolio and what grade I receive in this class?**

Yes. Your instructor will always be one of at least two portfolio readers of your work at the end of the term. If the second reader in the group agrees with your instructor about the grade for your portfolio, then that agreement will determine the grade you receive on the portfolio. If the second reader does not agree with your instructor, then a third reader will be asked to read your portfolio. If the third reader agrees with your instructor, then the grade stands. If the third reader agrees with the second reader, then your grade is based on the agreement of readers two and three. The goal is to arrive at a community grade rather than a grade based solely on one instructor's preferences.

3. **What happens if one person in the portfolio group grades much harder than the others? Doesn't this mean I'll probably get a low grade if that person reads my portfolio?**

No, not necessarily. If the second reader does not agree with your instructor, a third reader is asked to read your portfolio and decide which of the first two readers is closest to the standards that the portfolio group has agreed about during the semester. (See question #2.) The portfolio groups also work to discourage instructors from being "hard" or "easy." We strive to have all instructors arrive at a common understanding of what portfolios deserve which grades, grounding their judgment in our detailed grading descriptions.

4. Shouldn't each instructor grade his or her own students' work?

Each instructor does have a hand in grading their students' work, but the portfolio groups assure students that their grades are a reflection of community standards—departmental and university-wide.

5. How can the portfolio group grade my papers if they haven't seen the assignment?

Writing 150 is a course that is designed to give you practice and instruction in the various kinds of writing that you will be asked to do throughout college. All instructors design their assignments with that goal in mind. The portfolio group, therefore, wants to be general in their assessment of your writing. They want to look at three samples of your writing and describe the group of three as "excellent," "good," "average," or "below average or failing." The ideal is that this grade reflects what most professors would say if they picked up your portfolio and read it. We want your grade to be based on the general quality of your writing alone, not on how well the writing satisfies instructor-specific instructions.

6. My instructor said that I have to type single-space, have fewer than two sentence fragments, and underline the thesis statement in every essay just to get a C. If the portfolio group doesn't know this, then what happens?

Instructors often have minimum requirements that they want every paper to meet. For example, some say that a paper can't be handed in more than one day late. When instructors have such requirements that may not be the same as other instructors in the portfolio group, they will enforce those requirements by making sure you meet them before you submit a portfolio to the portfolio group at the end of the term. This way, everyone who reads your portfolio will assume it has met any instructor-specific minimum requirements. If you don't meet minimum requirements that your instructor sets, your instructor won't allow you to submit a portfolio at the end of the term.

7. Could two people in my portfolio group agree that I deserve a B and then my instructor give me a C anyway because of absences or class participation?

That should not happen. The portfolio grade is your letter grade for the semester. Typically you should not expect your grade to be adjusted—either up or down—by your instructor beyond a plus or a minus for the letter grade the portfolio group gives you. If your grade needs adjusting down, you probably didn't meet the minimum requirements (e.g., too many absences) and you should not have been allowed to submit a portfolio in the first place, meaning you would deserve an F. If an instructor over in Biology looks up your grade in WRT 150, they should be assured that this grade basically reflects how well you write, not your attendance, your improvement, or your good (or bad) attitude—as should also be true in your Biology class.

8. **Just looking at my portfolio at the end of the term doesn't show how much I've improved. Shouldn't my grade be based, at least in part, on my improvement?**

We do not believe it makes sense to grade on improvement itself. Your grade in WRT 150 should be based on the quality of your writing at the end of the term. This way, what counts as A, B, C, D, or F is the same for every student, or at least as close to being the same as we can manage. Instructors can adjust grades (usually with a plus or a minus) based on your participation, improvement, or other factors. "Improvement" itself is probably impossible to measure accurately even if we wished to do so. We hope that your improvement will earn its proper reward when we decide how well you are writing by the end of the term when you submit your portfolio.

9. **I like to have grades during the semester so that I know how well I am doing. I don't want my grade at the end of the term to come as a big surprise.**

We agree that you should know how you are doing, but we do not believe interim grades would be the most effective approach to that need. Your instructor will be reading your writing throughout the semester and responding to it with comments, personal conferences, endnotes, and suggestions for revision. Most 150 classes have tutors from the Writing Center that work with you and point out strengths and weaknesses in your writing. And many instructors will have you read and comment on other students' work. For most students, a grade is not necessary for early drafts because the proper focus is on what the paper could be, not on what it is. But if you want a grade on an assignment and your instructor has not given one, just ask. The instructor will be able to tell you where she thinks the paper falls within the range of A to F. The instructor will probably tell you what she and others in the portfolio group have been saying about writing like yours. Don't be surprised if the instructor says, for example, that some in the group might say C and she, or others in the group, might say B. Group members often disagree, especially early in the semester, about what is an A, B, C, or D. If the instructor says your paper is probably a low B or a C, your next question should be: "What could I work on in this paper that would improve it?" Your instructor should love this question and this should give you the feedback you need to feel encouraged to try making even a good paper better. In the end, if you simply do the best you can with a reasonable amount of hard work, your grade at the end will be the best that you can earn. The last thing any of us would want to do is to encourage students to stop working before they have achieved the best work they can manage.

10. It seems to me that the portfolio-grading system is all about judging final products. Aren't we supposed to be interested in the writing process?

Our first-year writing program does stress learning strategies and skills that help you develop your own writing process. In fact, because the portfolio group grading system focuses on what you can do at the end of the semester, it encourages and gives opportunity for every paper to be revised. Revision is the heart of the writing process. That is, we teach and value better writing processes because they do tend to produce better writing. In the end, we believe that grading your results keeps the best focus on learning to use writing processes effectively.

11. What is supposed to be in my portfolio?

Every student should submit three papers, including at least one with citations and references that show your ability to conduct scholarly research and use its results effectively. Ask your instructor if you are not sure. Your instructor and the other students should help you make good choices about what goes in the final portfolio.

12. Can I include a paper in my portfolio from another class?

No, unless you receive permission from the instructors of both classes and make arrangements with your WRT 150 instructor about what you can use and how you can use it. Without earlier arrangements like that, all papers in your portfolio must have been assigned and seen by your WRT 150 instructor, and they must be originally created for the class you are taking. Students who secretly submit work from another class (even an earlier WRT 150 class) violate the Student Code's provisions on academic honesty and integrity, a very serious matter. The results may include failing the course and being reported to the Dean of Students for further action.

RESOURCES FOR STUDENT WRITERS AT GRAND VALLEY

LIBRARY RESOURCES

The goal of library-related instruction in WRT 150 is to help you become an information-literate lifelong learner who can use academic and professional research methods and sources. In order to reach this goal, you will learn how to develop and implement a research strategy, locate the resources necessary to meet your information needs, and evaluate the information that you find.

Many WRT 150 instructors work closely with Grand Valley librarians and bring librarians into class to help you learn how to use Grand Valley's libraries and online library resources. In addition, each class has a designated library liaison who will work with you on your research for WRT 150. Ask your instructor for the name of your library liaison, or feel free to ask library staff to help you find the right person. Grand Valley librarians are eager and ready to help you search for and select the best sources for your paper, develop research questions, identify research strategies, evaluate the usefulness of specific sources, and find relevant and reliable information online. Library liaisons are available in person, by e-mail, or by telephone. Ask for their help.

Research consultants are also available to help you get started using the library's collection to write your paper. They are students themselves and are highly trained in sharing information literacy skills. The library's research consultants work alongside writing consultants and speech consultants in the Knowledge Market, which you can find in the GVSU libraries in Allendale and Grand Rapids. For more information or to schedule an appointment visit www.gvsu.edu/library/km.

COMPUTER CLASSROOMS

While we do use other schedules and plans, WRT 150 classes generally meet twice a week, once in a traditional classroom and once in a computer classroom. Computer classrooms are sometimes used simply for writing and revising drafts, but your instructor may introduce a range of activities—brief in-class writing exercises, peer review sessions, and research assignments, for example—to help you gain expertise in a range of writing skills and strategies.

Any Grand Valley computer that you use in a computer classroom gives you the option to save items to a personal drive (the "N" drive), or cloud drives (OneDrive or Google Drive). You can access items saved to your network account from various campus locations, such as other campus computer labs and some campus living quarters, as well as from other Grand Valley campuses. You can also retrieve items on the N drive from an off-campus home computer. You have access to your cloud drives through any device that has an internet connection on campus and off. Seek assistance from Grand Valley's IT office (616-331-2101) for more information about saving files.

The computer classrooms use recent versions of Microsoft Word for Windows as the primary word processing software. This means that Microsoft Works documents, Apple Pages documents, and other documents do not open in a computer classroom unless you have saved them in a compatible format like rich-text format (.rtf), which you can do with nearly any word processing program. It also means that documents prepared in the computer classroom will not open on some other computers, especially older computers, unless you have saved them in rich-text format or another format used on that computer. Your instructor may be able to suggest other programs and methods for working on the same files both at home and in a computer classroom.

THE FRED MEIJER CENTER FOR WRITING

Peer writing consultants work in all of the writing center locations as well as in WRT 098 and WRT 150 classes. Consultants provide helpful feedback, offer advice, model writing strategies, and ask questions in order to help students improve as writers. Consultants do not simply check grammar and mechanics, nor do they predict what grade a paper may receive. Essentially, the role of a consultant is to provide a well-trained pair of eyes to help writers think more critically about their own writing, provide reader feedback, and to assist writers in devising a plan for revision.

> "Talk to the writing consultants, ask your professor questions . . . They want you to be successful. Utilize them."
> —Bernadette J.

Most WRT 150 instructors use computer classrooms for consultations. In that setting, students have instant access to a consultant who can discuss any issue that may arise while you are working through writing activities or drafting and revising your papers. For example, you might need a quick discussion about the purpose of topic sentences, a guided tour through the library's many online resources for research, or a more in-depth conference about a whole draft. Make a point to seek out your writing consultant often. When you establish a working relationship with your writing consultant, they will come to understand your unique writing strengths and challenges, and can offer useful advice that is designed to help you with your current and future writing projects.

Consultants also will lead small-group discussions in WRT 150 classrooms. Small groups serve as a place to cultivate ideas, expand and clarify key elements, and devise a plan for a paper. The consultant's role in these situations is to help the group stay on track, encourage everyone's involvement in the discussion, model or prompt the group to use effective feedback strategies, and offer another perspective on your writing.

Here are some tips for making your group discussions work:

▶ Come prepared with specific questions or areas of your writing for which you need feedback.

▶ Bring enough copies of your draft for each student and the consultant to have one. This allows your readers to follow along and write comments on the papers, which you might find helpful later in your revision process.

► Solicit the advice of everyone in your group, not just the writing consultant. The more reader input you have, the better sense you have about how readers understand your ideas.

In labs or small-group discussions, consultants are there as a resource to work through your individual writing needs. Get to know your classroom consultants early in the semester, and consider visiting them outside of class, when they are on duty in the writing center (LOH 120) or at any of the other Fred Meijer Center for Writing locations, including the Allendale Knowledge Market (Mary Idema Pew Library), the Steelcase Knowledge Market (Steelcase Library—DeVos–Pew campus), and online through Google Docs. For a list of all available locations and services, as well as writing resources and how-to guides, please visit the writing center Web site: gvsu.edu/wc.

GOOD WRITING IN WRT 150

When we set out to choose portfolios to be published in this textbook, we don't try to anticipate which ones will serve as perfect models for future students. Instead, our goal is to select writers who understand their paper's purposes and seek to challenge themselves with complex, interesting, and timely topics. We look for writers who know what it is they are trying to accomplish in their work, and authors who keep their audience in mind as they write. We also wanted to offer you a range of styles, subjects, and assignments, so that you can see the variety of approaches students take to successfully accomplish their writing goals.

No matter what your assignment may be, the keys to good writing remain consistent—a solid sense of purpose, focus, and audience. In showcasing work from previous WRT 150 students, we hope to open up classroom dialogue about the content as well as the writing. We have chosen ten writers to showcase in this year's edition of the book, and each has something special to offer.

Before each student's writing, you'll find a brief description of the essays included, as well as an explanation of why the Guide's editors selected the portfolio—the strengths we saw and admired in each student's work. You'll also find reflections from the writers about their experiences as a student in WRT 150. They offer sound advice about strategies you might consider trying as a student in WRT 150 this semester.

PORTFOLIO ONE

BY HERSHEL R TUCKER

As a student in Professor Corinne Cozzaglio Martinez's class, Hershel R Tucker enjoyed the creativity that came with coming up with his own topics to write about, despite the sometimes narrow requirements of each assignment. Hershel's decision to write about familiar topics that he found interesting helped him practice the writing strategies students learn in WRT 150, such as how to make decisions about the structure and organization of his essays. According to Hershel, these skills have been especially valuable in the Philosophy and General Education classes he's taken at GVSU since completing WRT 150.

Hershel, a psychology major, used his own life experiences to generate ideas to research and write about. His first essay, "Aural Autonomy," was his favorite, because it allowed him to explore how his Walkman enabled him to find freedom through music as a teenager. Hershel's second essay, "Digital Trucking," examines a particular issue in his workplace that is becoming common across industries—the move from paper to digital records. His final essay, "Indivisible?," raises important questions about the state of political discourse in the United States that we think all readers, regardless of political persuasion, will find compelling.

Hershel's Advice for WRT 150 Students

The best advice I can give is to always have more questions than answers.

AURAL AUTONOMY

The 1980s and 90s were a time of amazing technological advances, many of which emerged from the entertainment industry. Nintendo revolutionized gaming twice during the 80s—first with the NES and again when it released the Gameboy. In the 90s, we witnessed the development of the World Wide Web and the "information superhighway". We saw the transition from dial-up internet connections to high-speed cable, and from rotary phones to cellular. Compact Discs and DVDs became affordable, and therefore popular, during the 90s, before the iPod came along around the turn of the millennium. This last example owes at least some small thanks to my favorite piece of nostalgia from the 80s, though—The Walkman, from Sony.

Created in 1979, by Akio Morita as a means of avoiding his kids' rock music (Michaud), The Walkman was actually a spin on existing technology that had been used by reporters for some time: The Pressman (Rossen). The new version was made with the express purpose of listening to music, however, whereas the Pressman was for the recording and playback of live audio. There turned out to be a big market for such a device—the company sold over 400 million Walkmans before discontinuing the product in 2010 (Rossen).

As for me, I have always been a big fan of music. So, when I received my very first Walkman for a birthday in 1988, I was probably more excited than I had any right to be. I imagine my mother regretted buying it for me, almost immediately. For the next five years, I had headphones blaring everything from Jazzy Jeff's scratch performances on *He's the DJ, I'm the Rapper*, to Guns and Roses' entire *Appetite for Destruction* album.

I picked up music from anywhere I could. I dubbed albums like *Licensed to Ill*, and *Pyromania*, from my sister's collection. My best friend let me borrow his copies of *Night Songs*, and *Slippery When Wet*. I recorded just about all the popular music of that era from the radio. I had my father connect the VCR to the radio so that I could record the soundtrack from the movie "Breakin'". I was so obsessed that I can vividly recall him getting frustrated with my constant requests for batteries and blank cassette tapes and declaring that he would have to take out a second mortgage on the house, if I kept it up.

That was the 1980s generation, in a nutshell, though. A kid growing up in those days only really needed two things: an NES and a Walkman. Everything else was superfluous. Food? Meh. Water? That was my least favorite level on literally every video game. Air? They didn't release their first album for another 10 years. Ok, so maybe an occasional box of Ecto Cooler and some Saturday morning cartoons rated on our must-have list, too.

The great thing about the Walkman, though, was that it gave us a freedom that generations before us really never had. We could enjoy music anywhere, anytime. During the decade of MTV, that was a big deal. Whether we were on the school bus, in a library, out for a walk or jog, doing homework, or on a family road trip, the headphones were strapped securely over our ears. While beatboxes were also popular at the time, they were not as truly portable as the Walkman. The headphones also allowed us to enjoy our music in a way that was mostly not obnoxious to the people around us. To an eight-year-old, that's an entirely new level of freedom—the kind that William Wallace was screaming for, at the end of *Braveheart*.

Sometime in the early 1990s, my Walkman finally gave out. When my mother got me a new one, I was shocked—*shocked*—when I realized that the new unit came with a graphic equalizer on the front and a "Bass Boost" feature. What sort of unholy demon contract must someone have signed to obtain this level of audio wizardry? "Straight Outta Compton" took on a whole new dimension. The myriad mixtapes that I had started collecting from Chicago and Detroit disc jockeys were suddenly all the more amazing. At that point, I had never set foot inside a night club nor attended a concert, but I imagined that *this* must have been what it was like...and it was all for me. It was my own personal Studio 54, clipped conveniently to my belt on the side of my hip.

In 1993, I entered a new stage in my relationship with the Walkman when my mother had an affair and divorced my father. A couple years later, she married the man she was having an affair with, and took me and my brother to live with our new step-family. I hated them. They were ultra-suburbanite, whereas I was an inner-city youth. Our lifestyles and personalities clashed, causing the

© Ben Gingell/Shutterstock.com

Figure 1 I'm pretty sure "MEGA BASS 2X Bass Expansion Circuit" is code for "electronic devil magic". I'm on to you, Sony. ("Sony")

step-father and I to have more verbal confrontations than I care to remember. I mean, the guy wore a sweater tied around his neck, for cripes sake. Unsurprisingly, I sank into depression. But, when things got really rough, the Walkman was there to help me escape. I could just slip the headphones on and tune out the rest of the world.

I listened to "So Many Tears" and "Me Against the World", by Tupac when I felt the need to wallow in my angst—like when the step-father would wear a speedo in public, for instance. When I wanted a pick-me-up, I would play club mixes from B96 in Chicago, or Nirvana, or even Jodeci. In 1995, I got a part time job cleaning offices, used the money I earned on a pair of big over-the-ear noise cancelling headphones, and cranked my "ignore the step-family and pretend they don't exist" game up to eleven.

I would pull the cans over my ears, grab a pen and my notebook and write for hours. The format in which I would write didn't particularly matter. Poetry, short stories, journal entries; they all served to get the thoughts and emotions out of my head and out into the world with no risk of drama. I would doodle and sketch and write, with Bjork or Aphex Twin as my muse. If I wasn't feeling inspired, at the moment, I would take a walk to the comic book store, and browse their newest offerings. I would read the adventures of Batman, The Incredible Hulk, Spawn, and every superhero in between. My favorite escape, however, was the small creek behind our house.

The creek snaked through a small wooded area, nestled into a shallow gorge that it appeared to have carved out for itself. An uprooted tree formed a bridge that connected one side of the gorge to the other. I would sit on that tree for hours, with one headphone can on my ear so that I could hear the music and the other pulled back so I could listen to nature at the same time. The sound of cicada and chickadees and woodpeckers and the bubbling of the water mixed with tunes from Portishead and DJ Shadow and Orbital to create the perfect habitat for reflection and introspection.

Today, sadly, my Walkman is no more. Gone are the days of use-specific gadgets, replaced by the era of miniature computers that want to be everything to everybody. The spirit of the Walkman lives on, however, reincarnated into its own little space within my mobile phone. It is there with me in the gym, amping me up for my workout with the sounds of Bassnectar, Disturbed, and Zeds Dead. It is there during quiet summer-evening walks, soothing me with the berceuse of Loreena McKennitt, Nouvelle Vague and Joe Bonamassa. Even as I write this paper, I sit with a pair of earbuds pumping orchestral tunes from various movie and video game soundtracks into my cerebrum, in the hopes of finding just a tiny bit more inspiration. Yes, the device may be gone, but like John McClane, old habits die hard. Sitting here as an adult, I have to wonder if Akio Morita, when he first conceived of the Walkman, could have ever guessed the impact he would have on countless people like me. Probably not. It was likely a simple yet happy side effect of wanting some peace and quiet, around the house. Now, as a parent of a teenager who loves death metal groups like Infant Annihilator, I can certainly empathize with that.

Word Count: 1407

Works Cited

Michaud, Jon. "Walkman Nostalgia." *The New Yorker*, Conde Nast, 17 July 2014, www.newyorker.com/books/double-take/walkman-nostalgia. Accessed 26 Mar. 2017.

Rossen, Jake. "A Brief History of the Walkman." *Mental Floss*, 1 July 2015, mentalfloss.com/article/65620/july-1-1979-sonys-walkman-changes-recorded-history. Accessed 03 Mar. 2017.

"Sony Walkman." *Shutterstock.com*, 10 Oct. 2017, https://www.shutterstock.com/image-photo/london-10102017sony-walkman-retro-personal-cassette-734329102?src=ZIC92xtxqNW1AIqZ5zfF0g-1-40.

DIGITAL TRUCKING

Beginning in August of 2017, the trucking company I work for, Grand Rapids Transport, will begin transitioning from paper logs to electronic logs (known colloquially as e-logs). Many drivers, particularly the older ones, are upset by this—my father even went so far as to retire from the industry, knowing that new federal regulations would require carriers to use an e-log system. Publicly, these drivers will claim that their distress is based around learning and using a new type of technology, when a perfectly useable analog method already exists. My 15 years in the industry tell me that my fellow drivers might be a bit disingenuous about the reasoning behind their reservations, however.

Every long-haul commercial motor vehicle driver is required to maintain a log of the hours he or she has worked and the miles he or she has driven each day (FMSCA 16). There are rules set by the Department of Transportation (DOT) and Federal Motor Carrier Safety Administration (FMSCA) that restrict the number of consecutive hours (8) a worker can drive without a break, how long a driver can work overall in a given day (14 hours), and how many hours a driver can have on-duty during a seven or eight-day period (70). These regulations are in place not only to protect the drivers from dispatchers who may otherwise overwork them, but also to protect everyone else on the roadways from truckers who are driving while fatigued.

The DOT rules are important, but many drivers see them as being overly restrictive. The rules effectively put a cap on how many miles a driver can cover in a week, and subsequently, the amount of money he or she can earn. I believe this is their real beef with the e-logs. While still utilizing the obsolete paper logs, drivers can "fudge the facts" to squeeze in more driving than they would have been legally allowed to do. They can even create multiple log books, each describing different versions of their work week to trick police and DOT officers into believing the drivers are running legally.

On the other hand, e-log systems do not allow for this type of revisionist history. As soon as a truck's wheels start moving, the system kicks in and changes the log status from "off-duty" to "driving." There is no option to cancel the status change, nor to alter it. Drivers cannot turn off the e-log device to keep it from recording his or her movement, either. If the truck is on, the device is on. That is why drivers are upset with the transition to the new system. It's not the change itself that they fear, it is the tightening of what they see as already stifling federal restrictions on their earning potential. While their concerns are certainly legitimate, I believe my fellow drivers' angst is directed toward the wrong target.

With the rapid and unending advancement of transportation technology, there is simply no way to avoid the use of e-logs. They offer trucking companies far too many advantages to be so easily dismissed. E-logs, for example, use GPS tracking to log where a driver was when they started their day, where they ended their day, and every stop in between. This gives companies the freedom to get a rough estimate as to where their trucks are, at any point in time. That is a huge benefit for a trucking company, because it gives them the capability to update freight brokers, shippers, and receivers with delivery times and freight locations. It also allows dispatchers to plan and book freight loads more efficiently.

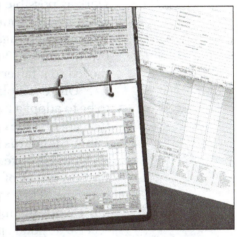

Electronic logs also provide drivers themselves with some benefits. First, once drivers are properly trained on one of the better electronic logging systems, e-logs can be substantially easier to maintain. They eliminate the need for other paperwork, as well, such as

Figure 1 An example of a paper log and trip report.

trip reports—papers in which a driver must record his miles driven within the borders of each state he or she visits. Figure 1 shows examples of paper logs and trip reports that a driver must complete throughout his or her workday. These are not the only style that drivers can use, as each company tends to have their own preferred templates, however no matter what style a company chooses, there are more similarities than differences between log and trip report templates. Ridding themselves of this kind of busywork is the type of automation drivers should welcome.

What these drivers should be railing against is the industry that accepts—and in some cases, requires—dispatchers to be dishonest and manipulative with the drivers to whom they are assigned. They should be protesting the self-same industry that lobbied for deregulation to get itself exempted from the Fair Labor Standards Act (Rodriguez et al, 207), creating a pay structure that incentivizes drivers to exhaust themselves when a simple pay increase would allow them to work a more manageable schedule, leading to less fatigue, less driver turnover and fewer crashes (Rodriguez et al, 222). As it stands now, company drivers are most often paid on a per-mile basis. This incentivizes drivers to cover as many miles as possible so that companies can optimize the drivers weekly output and compensate for other costs, such as truck lease payments— in other words, the current system is set up to squeeze as much work as possible out of drivers in the name of higher profits. It has often been a source of bewilderment for me that so many drivers willingly fight against safety regulations that would work in their favor, if the $726.4 billion industry (ATA) in which they worked moved to a fairer and more practical pay scheme?

One example of how the industry could do this, would simply to be to adopt a more traditional wage scale based on hours worked, instead of miles driven. Their current exemption from the Fair Labor Standards Act allows trucking companies to work drivers as much as is convenient for the company (within the aforementioned FMCSA hours of service regulations), without having to pay them overtime. This creates an environment in which drivers feel they must work the maximum number of hours each week, in order to receive a "good" pay check.

Beyond the obvious fatigue this can cause, driver health is also affected. According to the Center for Disease Control (CDC) and The National Institute for Occupational Safety and Health (NIOSH), 70% of drivers are obese and they are twice as likely as the average adult worker in the United States to have diabetes. Part of that problem stems from a lack of health education for drivers in the industry, part from lack of healthy food options while drivers are on the road; but the largest part of the problem, in my opinion, is the utterly sedentary nature of the job. Combine that with extraordinarily long work days, and it's a perfect recipe for poor health and obesity among working drivers.

As for the industry itself, the Owner-Operator Independent Drivers Association (OOIDA) is staunchly opposed to the government imposing requirements for electronic log use (Jailett). They believe that the regulation is in violation of the 4th Amendment, which disallows illegal search and seizure. However, the e-log does not show officers anything more than what should be on your paper logs, to begin with, so it is unclear how this regulation would be in violation of the Amendment. OOIDA has a more compelling case, however, when it argues that the regulation will hurt independent contract drivers with new costs they would not have otherwise had to pay (Jailett). The problem with this argument is that there are low-cost options available in the electronic logging systems market. If you have an Android or Apple device, there are several options available at no initial cost (Overdrive). Even if cheap options did not exist, however, all these costs are tax-deductible, making the point moot.

This is not to say that electronic log devices are a perfect solution. There are questions about driver privacy, for instance, that need to be addressed. However, technological advances are a constant in the transportation industry. In that light, and with employers looking to reap their many benefits, the change to electronic logging systems seem inevitable. To that end, C. William Pollard, chairman emeritus of ServiceMaster, teaches us that, "without change there is no innovation, creativity, or incentive for improvement. Those who initiate change will have a better opportunity to manage the change that is inevitable" (116). Pollard would likely advise drivers to take more of a leadership role in switching over to the new system.

Rather than fighting against the implementation of e-logs, drivers would be better served embracing the advantages these systems can offer them and leveraging those advantages to their own favor. Drivers stand to gain a lot from the new system: gains in health and fitness, decreases in nuisances such as paper busywork and daily check-calls from dispatchers and brokers, and perhaps even a restructure of the current pay schemes. Perhaps, then, it is time for drivers to end the witch hunt and begin thinking about how best to integrate this new technology into the current paradigm of his or her daily life.

Word Count: 1529

Works Cited

"ATA - ATA American Trucking Trends 2016." *ATA - ATA American Trucking Trends 2016*, American Trucking Associations, www.trucking.org/article/ATA-American-Trucking-Trends-2016. Accessed 15 Mar. 2017.

Federal Motor Carrier Safety Administration. "Interstate Truck Driver's Guide to Hours of Service." *FMCSA*, Mar. 2015. https://www.fmcsa.dot.gov/sites/fmcsa.dot.gov/files/docs/Drivers%20Guide%20to%20HOS%202015_508.pdf.

Jaillet, James. "OOIDA in latest legal filing: ELD mandate too costly, too intrusive." *Overdrive*, Overdrive Magazine, 21 Aug. 2016, www.overdriveonline.com/ooida-in-latest-legal-filing-eld-mandate-too-costly-too-intrusive/. Accessed 18 Mar. 2017.

Overdrive. "ELDs on the Market Today". *Overdrive*, Overdrive Magazine, 13 Mar. 2017. http://www.overdriveonline.com/2015eldchart/. Accessed 18 Mar. 2017.

Pollard, C. William. *The soul of the firm*. New York, HarperBusiness, 1996, p. 116.

Rodriguez, Daniel, Felipe Targa, and Michael H. Belzer. "Pay Incentives and Truck Driver Safety: A Case Study." *Industrial and Labor Relations Review*, vol. 59, no. 2, 2006, pp. 205-225, ProQuest Social Sciences Premium Collection, http://search.proquest.com.ezproxy.gvsu.edu/docview/60002587?accountid=39473.

INDIVISIBLE?

It has been years since I have spoken to my father about politics. It wasn't always this way—we used to talk about what was going on in Washington, all the time. Things went a bit awry, at some point, though, and what were once civil disagreements about policy became angry arguments about "fake birth certificates" and whether health care should be considered a basic human right. It occurred to me that all his information was coming from Fox News and right-wing talk radio. What I didn't know was that it was just as apparent to *him* that all my information was coming from the "liberal media."

So, sick of the bickering and guilt tripping and name calling, we decided to call a truce and put an end to the political talk. It was clear that we were on completely opposite sides of most issues, anyway. Plus, whenever we did manage to find common ground (for example, on campaign finance reform) we somehow ended up fighting about some technical detail of the issue. We decided that since neither of us were going to budge on our ideals—he was too old to change and I was a young know-it-all—there was really no point in arguing, anymore.

To Arthur Brooks, president of the American Enterprise Institute, the breakdown in dialogue between my father and me would likely be analogous to the political division and tension in the United States of America. There was a time when people from opposite sides of the aisle could work together toward a common goal. There was a time when we spoke to one another with respect. That time, sadly, is no more. We live in an age of extremes; an age in which a person can't espouse compassion for refugees without being called a "snowflake," an age in which one can't express concern for government overreach in the context of religious freedoms without being called a fascist, or a zealot. There's simply no middle ground, anymore. To quote Brooks, "It's unpleasant. It's not right." So, how did we get here?

We, the people, are the problem.

According to Alan Abramowitz, the Barkley Professor of Political Science at Emory University, the political polarization began with Nixon's "Southern Strategy," which was a concerted effort to pull white voters from southern states into the Republican Party. The division continued through the policies and rhetoric of the Reagan era, creating a snowball effect, which has led us to where we find ourselves today. Abramowitz argues that the politicians started by nudging their base toward more extreme directions, so that those votes would be easier to obtain.

However, Abramowitz continues, it was that very polarization, coupled with the electoral college voting system, that began to constrain politicians' ability to be centrist. Republican candidates must appeal to the most right-leaning constituents, in order to win their primaries. The same applies to Democratic candidates, except their appeal must be directed toward the more liberal portions of their constituencies. This, of course, leads to divisive rhetoric and a very "us versus them" type of mentality.

That sort of mentality, as it turns out, is not very difficult to cultivate in humans. Social psychologist Jonathan Haidt points to our innate predisposition toward tribalism as a cause of the increasing gap between left and right political factions (2016). It is visible in the racial divide we continue to witness in the United States, as well as the political and cultural gaps in this country. Using Haidt and Bjorklund's theory of the five moral values that define our political leanings (2007), it becomes a bit clearer as to the root cause of the division between tribes: we simply care about different things.

The innate moral values that humans are born with, according to Haidt and Bjorklund, include harm/care, fairness/reciprocity, in-group loyalty, authority/respect, and purity/sanctity. It is pretty easy to guess which political groups care more about each of those values. Liberals tend to care far more about harm/care and fairness/reciprocity than conservatives, and far less about in-group loyalty, authority/respect, and purity/sanctity (Haidt). In this way, liberals can be said to have a two-factor moral compass, whereas conservatives have more of a five-factor morality. Conservatives hold moral values that liberals simply do not agree are a part of morality (Haidt). Given these different senses of what constitutes morality, it is only natural for members of both sides to have difficulty in understanding their political counterparts on a fundamental level. This failure to understand one another inevitably leads to failures of communication and conflict.

A large part of the communication failure also has to do with a psychological phenomenon that has only recently been discovered by researchers Brendan Nyhan and Jason Reifler, at the University of Michigan. They call it the "backfire effect". When someone holds an incorrect belief strongly enough, presenting them with facts that disprove their belief may make them cling even more tightly to those fallacious beliefs.

Considering how many of the discussions with my father ended, Nyhan and Reifler's findings make sense to me. I often presented him with studies and articles with facts that contradict his arguments. Except, rather than internalizing this new data, he would simply dismiss the source as untrustworthy, regardless of their credibility. I imagine he felt the same frustration with me, when I scoffed at his quoting Bill O'Reilly. This is the reality of political discourse in America, today. Does that mean we are doomed to eternal animosity between the parties? What can we possibly do to bridge the political chasm that separates us even from those we love?

We, the people, can be the solution.

Brooks argues that the solution to the increasing polarization and distrust between the political left and right is simply to be more flexible and ambiguous in our ideology. His ideal would be to have conservatives who are "warriors for the poor" and liberals who extoll the virtues of free market enterprise. In other words, he wants us to move back toward political centrism.

This is a charmingly saccharin suggestion, but Brooks offers no insight on how we can achieve this. With political ideologues taking over the conversation on both sides of the aisle, and pushing the base of both major parties further to the left or right, how do we pull the base back toward the center? Perhaps, it begins with how we think about one another. If we understand Haidt and Bjorklund's theory of moral values, it becomes a little easier to empathize with your political opposite. Rather than being someone who we view as unintelligent or malevolent, we see them as someone whose values are different from our own. The conservative is not looking to deny minimum wage increases because he wants to keep people poor, but because he places a higher value on individual liberty—in this case, a company's ability to retain the fruits of its labor—than on the harm/care construct. On the other hand, a liberal does not protest for LGBT rights because she wants to force everyone in the country to share her beliefs, but because she prizes fairness values more than in-group loyalty and purity. When we think of our political differences in this way, we can begin to alleviate some of the animosity between the two ideologies.

The second part of the solution, I believe, is to change how we talk to one another. We ought to be having a political conversation, rather than an argument, in this country. Instead of the name calling and viciousness that has become so rampant in our society, we need discourse. Instead of knee-jerk reactions, we need measured responses. This, of course, is not to say that we must accept whatever foolishness the other side throws at us. That is the beauty of having diverse cultures and views in America: we balance one another out. When one side gets too extreme, the other needs to step up and pull them back to reality. Without the liberal value of fairness, we would not have the 40-hour work week and child labor laws. Without the conservative value of respect/authority, we would not have such a strong military.

As we have seen, liberals and conservatives differ quite a bit in the moral values they feel most strongly about. Perhaps, then, the best practice in persuading someone to accept our point of view is to appeal to their sense of morality. For example, a liberal attempting to persuade a conservative to support universal healthcare may have more success if they frame their argument from the perspective of in-group loyalty and purity, rather than harm/care. Similarly, a conservative attempting to convince a liberal of the importance of tax cuts might be better off arguing their point from a fairness perspective.

In addition, we should follow Haidt's advice and implement some of the conversational practices Dale Carnegie espoused in his book "How to Win Friends and Influence People." The first, and perhaps most important, step is to avoid criticizing the person with whom we are conversing (Carnegie). Finding common ground is another tactic that one should use, before making the more controversial point. Another important step is to build an exigency in their mind; Carnegie refers to this as arousing "an eager want" in the other person. Carnegie presents so many additional strategies that could prove useful when engaging in persuasive conversation of any sort that it is impossible to describe them all within these few pages; in my opinion, that only solidifies the book's "must-read" status for anyone who is interested in engaging in political discourse.

Of course, given Nyhan & Reifler's research, how we speak to one another may be moot. After all, how do you persuade the unpersuadable? In my opinion, however, we must behave as though the backfire effect does not exist. We must continue using facts and evidence-based reasoning in our discussions, regardless of their effect, or lack thereof, on the listener. We must debate our side of the argument to the best of our abilities, or risk allowing extremism to continue to spread across this country.

In the end, it falls upon us as individuals to correct our collective course. Only by working on ourselves—the way we think about others, the way we speak to others, and our willingness to persist in the face of absolute obstruction—can we bring back the bygone era of mutual respect between political opponents. We must change our political interactions starting, as Michael Jackson so harmoniously suggested, with the "Man in the Mirror." Perhaps it is fitting that our best solution comes not from the myriad political heavyweights, psychologists, and intellectuals weighing in on the matter, but from the man who sang to us about "Human Nature" in an attempt to "Heal the World."

Word Count: 1794

Works Cited

Abramowitz, Alan. "How did American politics become so polarized?" *Big Think*, http://bigthink.com/videos/how-did-american-politics-become-so-polarized.

Brooks, Arthur. "A conservative's plea: Let's work together." *Ted Talks*, Feb. 2016, https://www.ted.com/talks/arthur_brooks_a_conservative_s_plea_let_s_work_together.

Carnegie, Dale. *How to win friends and influence people.* Grahamstown, S.A. Library for the Blind, 1956.

Haidt, Jonathan. "Can a divided America heal?" *Ted Talks*, Nov. 2016. http://www.ted.com/talks/jonathan_haidt_can_a_divided_america_heal.

Haidt, Jonathan. and Fredrik Bjorklund. "Social intuitionists answer six questions about morality." *Moral psychology. Sinnott-Armstrong W (ed.).* Oxford University Press, 24 Apr 2007.

Nyhan, Brendan, and Jason Reifler. "When corrections fail: The persistence of political misperceptions." *Political Behavior* 32.2 (2010): 303-330.

PORTFOLIO TWO

BY DANA VANDYKE

Although some students don't feel like they have enough ideas for a complete essay, Dana VanDyke, a music major, had the opposite challenge. As a WRT 150 student, Dana found that her biggest difficulty was "learning how to condense [her] thoughts into concise sentences that gave the reader just the necessary information." But for Dana, the advice she received from her peers in Professor Teresa Gibbons' class made a huge difference, and she found that once she could learn to accept critiques from others and incorporate their feedback into her essays, her writing was stronger and more focused.

You'll see Dana's efforts to focus her writing in the three essays she submitted for her final portfolio. Her first essay, a narrative titled "Walking Among the Apple Blossoms" recalls how her relationship with her father evolved as she grew up on her family farm. Dana explores the psychology of lifelong learning in "How Can You Improve?" and her final essay, "Painful Playing," sheds light on the under-researched field of medical treatment for musicians with performance-related injuries. The editors were especially impressed by Dana's careful use of challenging, relevant sources; it's clear that Dana knew what she wanted to say and she used sources to support *her* argument and organization, rather than having the sources control what she wrote. As a result, her essays are clear, engaging, and effective, and strong models from which other WRT 150 students can learn.

Dana's Advice for WRT 150 Students

Write everything down as soon as it comes to your mind, even if it may not be exactly what you are looking to say in your paper. Choosing a topic can be one of the hardest things, but when you dig deep and find one that you feel strongly about, the writing will flow much more easily.

WALKING AMONG APPLE BLOSSOMS

The front door flew open and my dad ran inside. "Dana, I think I know what that smell is! Follow me," he said. My eyes widened in excitement as I quickly jammed on my boots and sprinted out the door. I followed my dad eagerly into the lower pasture that settled along the west side of our barn. For the past two weeks, my father and I had been searching for the alluring aroma that filled the air around our home, and we had finally found it: the apple blossom. It grew on trees that surrounded the edge of our creek, filling the lower pasture with a lively white glow, contrasted against the bright green leaves around it.

I grew up in a house that sat on twenty acres of land. Most of my neighbors were farmers, whether it was for a living or a hobby, and children were blessed with the freedom to explore the outdoors. Growing up on a hobby farm myself, some of my earliest memories consist of wandering through the creek bed and woods that surrounded our property. The pride of my siblings and me stood in the forts we built and the few critters we shot with our BB guns. I was the youngest in my family, with two older sisters and two older brothers. My dad owned a mechanic shop where he worked five days a week, while my mother stayed at home and lovingly tended to her children's every need. At the end of the day, my father always came home with a kiss for my mom and hugs for us all.

As soon as I could walk, I was out in the barn every day with my father when he came home from work. Before I was old enough to lift the shovel and muck out stalls, I simply followed him around, copying his every move. I was there with him when he started up the tractor and took it out to the field every spring to spread manure or bale hay. We both would sit on top of that tractor with our raggedy ol' barn clothes, baking in the sun as we drove round after round through the field. I was there to watch him spend hours fixing old machinery that refused to start, only to have it break down in the middle of field again and again. I was there with him when he stayed up late, working with all his might to help a pregnant cow deliver her calf, at times only to reap a stillborn calf or a dying mother. But I was also there with him to share the pride and accomplishment of healthy newborn calves, beautiful green pastures, and a barn loft full of hay each year, and he was there for me when I began to discover my own love for farming, a bond that made us inseparable.

Around the age of six, I could finally lend a helping hand in the barn, where every day I helped feed the animals and clean stalls. My oldest brother and I were the only two siblings who stayed actively involved in the farm, but by the time I was old enough to work, he was in college and too busy; so it was just me and my dad, every day. My dad began to refer to me as "the little farm girl he finally got" after five children. It always made me so proud to hear him say that.

"This is it, Dana! Smell this!" my dad said in excitement as he handed me the small flower he had picked from the nearby trees. I brought the flower to my nose and took a deep breath in, followed by a long exaggerated sigh. "Sure enough!" I said with a wide grin, "That's the smell." Spring had just begun, carrying with it the blooming of the beautiful grasses and trees around our small farm. Although every season brought forth its own share of beauty in the fields, I looked forward to the coming of spring the most. This was when we discovered our flower, and because of this very flower, my father and I began our weekly walks together.

Every Sunday afternoon after chores were finished, my father and I would make our way around the pastures surrounding the barn to check up on the grazing cows and the condition of the fields. On these walks, I began to notice the different sides of my dad: his intelligent side gave me insight to tasks such as soil health and herd management, and his curious side led us to discover a beautiful snowy owl that lived in the old oak tree behind our barn. His witty side taught me how to laugh at my own self for stepping in a cow pie, his caring side helped me out of the creek when my boot got stuck a foot deep in the mud, and most importantly his loving side always took the time to ask me about my week. Between all the joking and exploring, we always made time to fantasize about our dreams for our farm.

However, growing up on the farm also came with a lot of responsibility. I was quite busy as an eight-year-old, juggling school, piano lessons, and barn work, which included preparation for the yearly fair. In addition, in 2008 I faced a year full of changes that shook my life. In the spring of 2008, my oldest sister, Faith, got married and moved out of the house. Faith was the epitome of perfection, and although I was very happy for her, the thought of her leaving the house for good hurt me. It felt like a part of our family was missing. Only a few months later, my grandfather died. He had a very close relationship with every one of my siblings, and when we visited him in Iowa each year, he always had a jar full of candy waiting for us. Coping with his death was hard for the entire family. Facing these changes made me feel out of control in my life and I needed something to make me feel stable; I needed something to take my mind away from it all. Because I was known as the 'happy girl' by my parents and friends, I felt ashamed to show any sign that I wasn't still happy; so instead of talking about my feelings, I found other ways to deal with the pain.

It started as a simple goal to lose weight. I thought that maybe if I could just be a little more perfect, I would feel happy again. I was by no means an overweight girl, but with the societal pressures of the ideal image looming around me, I viewed myself as fat. But no matter how much I exercised or how little I ate, I was never skinny enough and still not happy. Quickly my desire for perfection led to an obsession to lose as much weight as I could, as fast as I could. I had never faced an internal difficulty like this before, so I was unaware of the severity of my situation. But it soon became a concern to others around me who began to notice. My dad sensed that my smile was no longer met with a sparkle in my eyes, and the joy in my laugh was fading. When I came home with a full lunch pail, my mother questioned me so I resorted to throwing my lunches away at school instead. At home I ate less and less, spreading food out on my plate and hiding it in my napkin. My obsession with my figure grew stronger each day. When my parents first noticed all of this, they lovingly pulled me aside and questioned my actions, ensuring not to be accusatory or make me feel targeted. But as time went on and I continued to eat less, they watched me even closer and asked more questions, and I felt the trust between my father and me slowly fading.

For fear of being imperfect and possibly letting my father down, I began bottling my feelings up inside me instead of talking to my dad like I usually did. My father became more upset, unwilling to let his daughter waste away in front of his eyes, yet unsure about how to help me. The subject of our walks became a conversation about my eating instead of the farm, and with my mind focused only on how I could lose more weight, my interest in what my dad had to say dwindled. That spring when my dad and I wandered down to the creek bed to marvel at the smell of the apple blossoms, it wasn't the most important thing to me anymore. With my energy level plummeting, I also got tired more quickly and sometimes our walks were even cut short. The more I realized these things, the more frustrated I got with myself and the more I began to withdraw. The more isolated I became, the more concerned my dad became. I found myself in a never-ending cycle of trying to be the perfect weight while sustaining a healthy relationship with him, but the weaker I became, the less time I spent with him.

Weeks turned into months until my condition was too much for my parents to handle. A year after this all started, my parents received a phone call from my fourth grade instructor, telling them that I had been throwing my lunches away every day at school. I vividly recall the deep, empty feeling in my stomach when my parents approached me about it. I pretended that it was nothing and apologized, but I could tell they weren't buying it. Exactly one week later, I came inside from the barn and heard my mother talking on the phone. From the quiet, grievous tone in her voice, I knew immediately. She had called the hospital. Blood rushed to my face as I angrily ran up the stairs, dashed into my room and slammed the door. *I can't believe they're actually doing this. How dare they!* I lay quietly in my bed for a few moments, frantically trying to come up with a plan. When I heard her finally hang up the phone, I marched downstairs, ready to fight back. But as I reached the bottom of the stairs, I stopped cold at the sight of my parents in a tearful embrace. Immediately all the angry thoughts of deception and betrayal rushed away, and I fell into their arms. Not a word was spoken for several minutes. We let the tears fall.

I was more scared that day than ever before in my life. On the ride to the hospital, my parents repeatedly assured me that everything was going to be ok. But my panicked thoughts drowned out their voices. *What did my dad think of me now? Not his perfect little farm girl now am I.* I was deathly afraid that I had ruined my relationship with my dad. After we arrived at the hospital and had a few tests done, my dad asked me to take a walk. We made our way out of the hospital doors and into the large parking lot outside. Decorative trees and bushes lined the sidewalks, and a soft breeze chilled my frail body. But the sun was still out, and even though the scenery wasn't as beautiful as back home, it was good enough. We walked in silence for several minutes; the last thing either of us wanted to talk about was the present. Soon my dad's gentle voice broke the ice, and we found ourselves lost in conversation about the farm as if none of this was happening. With little energy left in my body, we found a nearby curb and sat down. As we were talking, a small white flower blew onto the parking space in front of us. I gasped and looked over to my dad in disbelief. He looked back at me with a big grin, and shook his head. "Wow. Can you believe it? The apple blossom followed us all the way here." That was the first time I had smiled for real in a really long time.

Just a few hours later I was officially diagnosed with anorexia. I was to stay in the hospital for a minimum of a week, then continue as an outpatient as needed. My time at the hospital was totally different from anything I had experienced before, and at first I hated it. Away from everyone and everything I had ever known, I was forced to eat more food than I wanted to, and my level of activity was limited to virtually nothing. For the first few nights I cried myself to sleep, but as the days went on, I started to feel stronger. Every day I met with a therapist to talk about my feelings and participate in support groups, which helped me, realize that I was not the only one struggling with anorexia. My parents visited me every day, and each time my dad would comment on how much better I was looking, bringing me detailed updates on the farm. Thinking back on those conversations, I now realize that his effort in keeping the subject of our conversations away from my situation was his attempt at taking the guilt and shame of my problems away from me.

I was discharged from the hospital after nine days. I was terrified of what would happen after I left the hospital, but I was more excited to get back home to the farm. The very first thing I wanted to do was go on a nice long walk with my dad. But because of the strict exercise limits given to me, our walk was limited to the side of the barn. There were no apple blossom trees there. I could hardly contain my anger and disappointment; *Don't the nurses know what this means to me? Don't they know this is the one thing I'm looking forward to since the first day in the hospital?* But as the gentle spring breeze brushed against my face and the grass curved around the edge of my boots, my frustration faded and I began to relax. I finally felt safe at home with the familiar barnyard smell in the air and beautiful sight of grazing cattle in front of me.

After that day, the hardest part of my journey began: my road to recovery. I spent almost two full years going to regular doctor, nutritionist, and therapist appointments, while sticking to a strict meal plan every single day. It was hard work and often very painful for both me and my parents. There were times when I was doing very well, and times when I began to slip again. When I was ten, my dad caught me hiding some food under my plate, and before I knew it, he and I were in a heated argument, both of us saying things we knew we would regret. I went to bed early and very bitter at my dad that night. The next day at school after recess, I opened my locker to find a mini horse calendar with a small apology note from my dad about the night before; there was no way I could stay mad at him. He was never the one to let disputes go unsettled. This was just one of the many ways in which my parents demonstrated their patience and love for me throughout what would be over five years of recovery time.

Through all the ups and downs, I was surprised at how little my relationship with my dad changed, as it only served to grow stronger. The more I improved, the more I was able to work in the barn, the longer walks with my dad became, and the happier I became. The happier I became, the happier he became, and the stronger we both became, giving me the drive and will to battle harder against anorexia. Today, I am fully recovered, thoughts of food rarely enter my mind, and my relationship with my dad is stronger than ever. Although our lives are constantly changing, and we face difficulties of business that threaten to draw us apart, what we have been through keeps us together. And every spring since the day we first discovered the apple blossom, my father and I have taken time to walk down to the creek and smell the apple blossoms. And every time I pick that flower, I remember our long journey, and am assured that no matter what lies ahead, my father will be by my side, walking with me through it all.

Word Count: 2798

HOW CAN YOU IMPROVE?

Eduardo Briceño is a dedicated learning expert, international speaker, writer and promoter of a more focused learning environment in the educational system. Briceño was born and raised in Venezuela, then came to the United States where he earned a bachelor degree in both economics and engineering from the University of Pennsylvania and a master's degree in Education from Stanford University. After working in the Silicon Valley, he founded Mindset Works, a company with the goal of promoting a growth mindset in the educational and professional systems around the globe ("Why you should listen"). In November of 2016, Briceño gave a Ted Talk in Manhattan Beach, California, entitled "How to get better at the things you care about." Here he shares with his listeners how to improve in the areas of life that are most important to them.

Briceño begins his talk by addressing why it is so common to remain stagnant in our jobs and responsibilities, despite our hard work. Although we might spend hours doing something, many of us still seem to make little progress. According to Briceño, research shows that after about two years in a profession, performance plateaus. Because when we think we have become good enough, we stop spending time in the "learning zone," and focus only on the execution of our everyday job in the "performance zone." In the learning zone, the primary focus is to improve. Mistakes are welcomed as a way to make us aware of what skills we haven't mastered yet, enabling us to focus on smaller activities designed to improve those skills. On the contrary, the performance zone is focused on executing what we have already mastered, at the highest level possible. The goal in this case is to minimize mistakes. This zone seeks to perfect the immediate performance, whereas the learning zone focuses on developing certain skills, which will maximize our abilities and ultimately lead to a better performance ("How to get better").

To demonstrate the effect of alternating between these two zones, Briceño gives an example. A popular political leader and famous orator of ancient Greece, Demosthenes, did not become famous by giving speeches over and over in front of a crowd; this would be his performance zone. Instead, he designed ways for practicing the skills he needed to improve on, for example studying logics, law, philosophy and acting. He even built an underground room where he could practice without being disturbed and work on bad habits such as lifting his shoulders when he spoke. To fix this habit, he practiced in front of a mirror with a sword hanging over his shoulder as a painful reminder not to raise his shoulders. He also practiced speaking with stones in his mouth to improve the clarity of his speech that was suffering due to his lisp. In addition to this, he would practice giving speeches by the ocean to get used to the noise of large crowds he knew he would face. All of this he practiced during his time off stage, which eventually enhanced his ability to move a crowd.

Briceño spends time expanding on the deliberate practice demonstrated by Demosthenes. Deliberate practice, he explains, involves breaking down our abilities into smaller sub-skills that we can focus on and use to constantly push ourselves just beyond our comfort zone. Self-reflection on our own work and constant feedback from experts around us is crucial for making adjustments, and through time and repetition, improving our skills. According to Briceño, it is proven that those who are the best in their profession properly handle well the alternation between the learning and performance zones. The best salesman, he points out, will not simply go about making sales over and over, but will seek out more information, meet with consultants, learn new strategies, and test them to better their ability to make sales. Chess players don't spend all of their time playing games of chess, but strategize how to overcome specific moves they may face. This can be applied to all areas of profession. Unfortunately, because of the high-pressure society we live in which stresses consistent perfection, we often don't feel safe making mistakes and thus spend no time in the learning zone, explains Briceño. Spending all our time in the performance zone drastically limits growth and in the end hurts our performance.

In conclusion, Briceño gives examples of how to foster an awareness of this issue in everyday life, and train ourselves to spend more time in the learning zone with proper goals and expectations. We must first create for ourselves and coworkers a low stakes environment where the pressure of perfection does not inhibit mistakes from being made and openly discussed for development. We must lead as an example to others by talking about our mistakes, and by asking others for feedback on our strengths and weaknesses. This is exactly what psychologists call a "growth mindset", explains Briceño, wherein we believe that we can improve, want to improve and have an idea how to improve. We must be ongoing learners willing to explore endless areas of improvement in order to get better about the things we care about, because if there is a clear understanding of when we need to be in the learning and performance zones, possibilities for progress are endless.

This overarching concept of a "growth mindset" has made a significant impact on my life. As a piano performance major at Grand Valley, I constantly alternate between the learning and performance zones. Everyday practice requires full focus in the learning zone, but when playing in my lesson to demonstrate my progress each week, or collaborating with other musicians, I must be in the performance zone. Recently, my piano professor addressed my need to improve more quickly in my pieces from week to week. I was astonished and rather discouraged since I already was practicing over four hours a day. Out of frustration, my immediate reaction was to practice more. But then I remembered a book that my sister had introduced me to: *Mindset: The New Psychology of Success* by Carol S. Dweck. Recalling this, I began to deeply evaluate my state of mind every day as I practiced. I quickly realized my tendency to run through my songs over and over, without working on the specific passages my instructor would assign. Why was I doing this? I was afraid of making mistakes. Over the years, I had trained my mind to stay in the performances zone, focusing my daily practice on avoiding mistakes rather than learning and improving from them. I was one of many musicians surrounded by a high-pressured environment in the performance arts, and needed to learn when to think like a performer and when to think like a learner. Having come to this conclusion, I began focusing on small details such as finger/hand position, and worked deliberately on smaller passages for long periods of time. Only then did I receive the recognition for improvement that I had been working so hard towards.

"There are two distinct mindsets which can determine whether you become the person you want to be and whether you accomplish the things you value," states Carol S. Dweck, a professor of psychology at Stanford University. Dweck was the first to discover the growth mindset, and in 2006, wrote a book on it entitled: *Mindset: The New Psychology of Success*. In her book, she explains why people can have different mindsets that lead them to operate in one or the other zones more often. The "fixed mindset" is the belief that our qualities such as our abilities, personality and morality are predetermined. When people are told that they have certain abilities, they naturally seek to perform at their highest level at all times to prove their ownership of those qualities. This mindset is quickly instilled into children in school when they are told they have "talent" or are "smart." This leads children to strive after one goal in every situation: to prove themselves as being exactly what they were told to have been (6). As a result, when challenges arise, they are too afraid to make mistakes for fear of being de-labeled as the "untalented" or "dumb" kid. In their minds, qualities are either all or nothing, thus any feedback about their abilities is skewed into being either good or bad, and nothing in between. One can imagine how devastating it would be, then, to receive negative comments; for the fixed mindset, such words would mean they are no longer identified as being a certain trait, and working towards improvement in that area would be useless. In the end, those with this mindset never give themselves a chance to learn and improve, and their success is severely limited (7).

The "growth mindset," on the other hand, views one's traits not as something you are handed to live with the rest of your life, but as the beginning point for advancement. Although every individual's qualities are different from the start, the growth mindset does not see qualities as fixed, but improvable through work and effort. Those with this mindset have a goal not to prove over and over their possession of certain abilities, but rather to reach their fullest potential through mistakes and revision (7). They are willing to face challenges and fight through difficulties without a fear of mistakes, understanding fully that being willing to learn is the necessary key for advancement. Criticism of one's work is then welcomed, and the possibilities for what one may become are boundless (11).

I grew up surrounded by a fixed mindset community, where parents and instructors would tell children they were a "good girl" or "gifted," based on small accomplishments in the child's life. Although unintentional, this intuitively defined those who were not praised for their actions as "bad" or "dumb." I was the "talented pianist," so that meant it came naturally to me. I accepted what I was told and became comfortable with my abilities, unaware that continued learning was necessary for improvement. Family and friends would call me "the next Mozart" and expected me to play perfectly whenever they asked. One night, after I performed a piano solo at my choir concert in my junior year of high school, a woman came up to me and said, "Honey, you have such a rare and incredible talent. Very few are as talented as you. Never give it up." At the time, this was very encouraging and quite satisfying.

But the more I embraced these comments, the more worried I became about maintaining my title. As a result, I worked extra hard to ensure I made as few mistakes as possible at all times, subconsciously placing myself in the performance zone. Since I lacked the proper time in the learning zone, I failed to improve my playing in order to perform successfully, especially when faced with challenging piano pieces. I would learn difficult pieces by playing them through hundreds of times, praying for fewer mistakes the more I played them; the entire time I would hardly ever stop to work on the passages I was struggling with. The more I continued in the performance zone, the less improvement I made and the more frustrated I became. Soon, I began to feel pain in my hands and discovered I had injured myself from all my playing; I felt as if I had betrayed myself. I started to question my pianistic abilities and my plans for continued piano studies in college. *Maybe I don't really have the talent for it*, I said to myself. *There's no way naturally talented people have to work this hard, and they certainly don't hurt themselves.* But despite this temptation to give up, piano was what had defined me, and I couldn't imagine the shame of everyone realizing I wasn't really a "naturally talented" pianist.

Fortunately, I continued piano, and now that I have gained this valuable knowledge, I understand how I had been blocking my perception of my abilities and potential for the future. I failed to recognize that I was not born with a rare, fixed amount of talent; instead, piano was something I chose to work hard at from an early age, and that was the source of my talent. I am now a performing pianist in college and am faced with limited time to learn increasingly difficult pieces; this forces me to spend more time in the learning zone and less time in frustration from "disproving" myself in the performance zone. I now see that the potential for learning and improving is never-ending, but to unlock that, I needed the correct perspective.

A few years ago, Briceño wrote an article, "Growth Mindset: Clearing up Some Common Confusions" in *Mindshift Magazine*, where he gives examples of how peers, parents and instructors can raise children with a growth mindset. First, we must have the correct mindset ourselves: only then can we be an example to children. The next step is to praise children for hard work. If we tell children they are smart and leave it at that, when they face failure later in their lives, they will conclude what I concluded in high school: that their ability is not very high after all. In the end, they lose their confidence due to our words, instead of gaining it. But as Briceño made clear in his TED talk, even with hard work, many of us still fail to improve. So, we must take it one step further and coach students on how to think more deeply, because only then can they get smarter at working. For example, if students are working very hard but not improving at all, it would be useless for a instructor to praise them for their efforts without giving them strategies for more effective work. Students need a healthy awareness of what and how to improve in the most efficient and rewarding way, allowing them to become self-learners and gain independence. In the end, students will have a better foundation with the understanding that their abilities are not set in stone, but that smart, hard work in any area of their life will lead them to succeed.

Since I began to adopt a growth mindset, I have advanced significantly, becoming more successful in my performances and satisfied with my current yet developing abilities as pianist. With my career goal as a performer and instructor set very high, every bit of this knowledge will carry me through the hard work to come. When performances don't go my way, I will know not to give up, but to carefully study my mistakes, work on them by spending time in the learning zone, and do better at my next performance. As I face more performers who are better than me, and thoughts of not being "truly talented" creep in, I can push them aside and be confident that with work, I can become just as good. As a future instructor, I will also be able to recognize these two mindsets in my students, and encourage the growth mindset that will lead to happier, more successful lives.

Briceño begins his article, "Growth Mindset: Clearing up Some Common Confusions," with a simple, yet crucial statement that Dweck also makes: "the only way to be in the learning zone, is to have a growth mindset." This clearly summarizes the concept of the growth mindset. Only by having the correct understanding of what our abilities actually are, can we change our habits into those that will lead to progress. And when we truly believe our abilities can and will be improved, a love for learning is created. And with a love for learning, one will spend more time learning and reap more success. An awareness of this and the influences that an environment places on our minds is the answer to improving in the areas we care most about. If we continue to create an environment that rewards hard, thoughtful work and accepts mistakes as the way forward, we will foster a surprisingly successful generation.

Word Count: 2668

Works Cited

Briceño, Eduardo. "Growth Mindset: Clearing up Some Common Confusions." *MindShift: How we learn,* 16 Nov. 2016, kqed. org/mindshift/2015/11/16/growth-mindset-clearing-up-some-common-confusions/.

---. "How to get better at the things you care about." *TED,* November 2016, ted.com/talks/eduardo_briceno_how_to_get_better_at_the_things_you_care_about.

---. "Why you should listen." *TED,* November 2016, ted.com/talks/eduardo_briceno_how_to_get_better_at_the_things_you_care_about.

Dweck, Carl S. *Mindset: The New Psychology of Success.* Random House Publishing Group, 2006.

PAINFUL PLAYING

Joy and contentment wash over me as my fingers run across the piano keys. In my own little world, I feel myself breathing to the beat of the music and singing to the tune of the melody in my head. For ten years, I have been playing, and it is now a part of me. But suddenly, pain. Panic, doubt and terror rush over me as I desperately massage my hands, crying, praying for the pain to go away. But no relief, a pianist's nightmare. I had become injured from playing piano, no longer felt the same joy as I once did, and my dreams of a career in the performing arts faded. Millions of musicians face the very same injuries that end countless careers, yet the knowledge for preventing and treating them is lacking. Both music educators and health care providers must understand the psychology and physiology of the performing arts to prevent and properly treat performance-related injuries.

I was never warned about injuries related to my piano playing. In my lessons, my instructors focused on learning and remembering notes, and then we moved on. All my life I was told that my ability to play the piano was a certain "talent" given to me, as if it was something I was just born with. My natural response to this was that I must do everything right, so, as my workload on the piano increased and pieces became more difficult to master, I simply worked harder. But improper playing technique drove me straight into pain. Unaware that musical injuries even existed, I figured "pain was gain," and continued playing like I always had. But soon the fine motor skills in my hands began to slow, one of my fingers began to stiffen up like a rusty hinge, and the pain became unbearable. Too afraid to express my pain to my instructor and elders for fear of letting them down, I set up numerous appointments with doctors and hand specialists to find the answers.

Unfortunately, for months I never received the answers I was looking for. None of the doctors asked further questions about my career plan, but instead bombarded me with sundry opinions, including arthritis, muscle fatigue and overuse. I was recommended to take Ibuprofen to numb the pain and go through physical therapy only if I felt I needed it. This was near the end of my senior year in high school, and as I prepared for a recital and several other performances, my work on the piano only got harder. I fought my way through the pain, but by June, I could no longer ignore it. Desperate for answers, I searched the internet, and I finally found the information I needed. Through foundations such as Performing Arts Medicine Association (PAMA) and Health Promotion in Schools of Music (HPSM), I educated myself on all aspects of performance-related injuries, and diagnosed myself with Carpal Tunnel Syndrome (CTS). I learned that the most common causes for CTS are unhealthy repetitive motions with the fingers and hands that leads to tendon inflammation in the wrist. This irritates the main nerve that runs between the tendons, causing pain, tingling and weakness in the hand. Knowing this made me terrified about the future, but I knew I had to face the facts; so, for the next couple weeks, I dedicated my time to reading about recovery methods. But I still did not find the relief I was hoping for. I even mustered up the nerve to tell my piano instructor, but our only solution was to end lessons.

By mid-June, I had worthless hands, an empty piano bench and a broken heart. I had recently been accepted into the music program at Grand Valley, but at this point, college in the fall seemed impossible. As a last resort, I emailed the piano professor at Grand Valley to explain my situation, and the next day, she emailed back. Rows of tears streamed down my face, and the heavy weight of failure lifted from my shoulders as I read her story of working through CTS the summer before her piano studies at Juilliard University. She told me to take a break from piano for the summer to let the swelling go down in my wrists, and introduced me to the Alexander Technique. The Alexander Technique is a mind/body approach to understanding how to operate our bodies the way they were designed to work. The leading causes of performance-related injuries are unnatural movements with the body, whether it be slouching over a piano, tilting the neck to hold a violin, or singing with an extended neck. These actions put extra force on parts of the body that were not meant to carry the weight, causing the body to tense to compensate for the extra burden. Such tension for extended periods of time leads directly to injury. The Alexander Technique focuses on working through these bad habits by retraining one's brain and body to execute natural, organic motions; motions that are healthy for the body to do.

For three months while I was off the piano, I took Alexander Technique lessons from a certified instructor, who emphasized the basics of how my bones and muscles worked together. I began with learning how to sit and stand correctly, then slowly moved to walking. It was a slow process, sometimes taking an hour just to sit in a chair properly without my old habits taking over. But the results I got were unreal; the amount of tension I was causing by a misunderstanding of my body was not only limiting me in my pianistic abilities but also in everyday tasks. I discovered the link between my spinal alignment and arm tension that had led to CTS, and found that my stiff finger was "trigger finger", caused by tension held in my index finger through complex passages on the piano. This had been working directly against the natural movements of the hands. But through these lessons, I learned how to correct my bad habits and discover a remarkable ease of movement.

My professor kept in contact with me throughout the summer and gradually transitioned me back onto the piano. In the first few lessons, we began by stretching for several minutes, starting with the toes and working our way up to our fingertips. This helped me become aware of my entire body, reminding me of its important roles for efficiency in movement. As I sat down on the piano bench, we applied the Alexander Technique to the piano. She instructed me on how to position my legs beneath me for optimal support, how to hold my torso so that I lifted my arms from my back muscles instead of shoulder joints (which are only meant for rotation, NOT for physically lifting the arm), and how to properly align my arms, wrists and fingers with the keyboard. After several lessons, she stressed smaller details such as how each of the fingers operated in different ways, and where each finger should be positioned on the keys according to its individual strengths and weaknesses. The work was slow and hard, taking me hours in small ten minute sessions for several months to retrain my body how to work correctly at the piano. But every bit of information made a world of difference, allowing me to accomplish passages comfortably. Although the information I had initially found online had helped me mentally, one-on-one lessons with a instructor to demonstrate was the only way I would recover. As complicated as this may seem, I know that I'm not the only musician who has walked this path.

According to a national survey done in 1986 by the International Conference of Symphony and Orchestra Members (ICSOM), "orchestral musicians have one of the highest rates of occupationally-produced pain" (Horvath 102). This is because musicians push their bodies to the limit for hours at a time to perfect their skills, but little knowledge is available to treat their unique needs. Unfortunately, this is still the case today. Laura M Kok, an orthopedic at Medisch Centrum Alkmaar, a highly-acclaimed hospital in the Netherlands, confirms this. Her recent studies have found that up to 90% of adult musicians complain of regular musculoskeletal conditions during their career (487). Since 2013, issues related to the skeletal and neuromuscular systems have been reported in up to 50% of musicians, according to Santiago Toledo, a primary physician at the Rehabilitation Institute in Chicago (S72).

But when did this become such a big issue? Judy Palac, instructor of violin and associate professor of music education at Michigan State University has published several articles in this area of research. In one of her articles, she gives a brief summary on the history of performance-related injuries and how they have plagued musicians for centuries. Letters and diaries have been collected from the 18th century and following, confirming that virtuosos such as Franz Liszt, Sergei Rachmaninoff, Glenn Gould, Gary Graffman, Ernestine Whitman and Leon Fleisher faced moderate to severe injuries that forced them either to take years of leave from their performing careers, or end their careers altogether (as was the case with young pianist Robert Schumann) (Palac 878). It was around the 18th century that the technical level of repertoire was increasing and instruments were being altered with additional keys and harder action; this took a toll on the bodies of musicians. Without the advanced knowledge of the body and technical concepts necessary for musicians to operate these instruments, pedagogy in the schools did not change quick enough and injury resulted. According to Toledo, musicians were afraid to speak about their pain for hundreds of years, being frequently named "overly-sensitive" or even deserving of the pain due to the limits to which they pushed their bodies (S73). It was not until the mid-20th century when famous pianists Gould and Graffman became seriously injured that musicians at all levels felt comfortable enough to come out about their pain. Studies were then conducted and the first official documents on pedagogy were updated based on their findings (Palac 879).

There are numerous types of injuries that musicians can face, the most common being severe muscle tension, tendonitis, carpal tunnel syndrome (CTS), trigger finger, and focal dystonia. All of these, in the most basic sense, are results of an improper understanding of how our body operates in its most natural form. But such knowledge is crucial for setting the foundations of proper technique on our instruments. Improper technique may include incorrect embouchure (placement of the mouth around a mouthpiece) in brass and wind players, improper arm, wrist and hand movements in string and percussion instruments, or overall harmful body posture (Dommerholt 128). LM Kok, health specialist at Northwest Hospital Group in the Netherlands, emphasizes that years or even months of repetitive motions in these unnatural positions causes injuries, and in many cases, musicians that face this are told they are unable to return to their career. This is an astounding and rather frightening reality. Yet as common as these problems are, so much behind these injuries remains a mystery, and more and more young musicians are entering college with pre-existing problems (488).

Kris Chesky, board member of the Health Promotion in Schools of Music (HPSM) foundation, further explains in his article, "Health Promotion in Schools of Music: Initial Recommendations for Schools of Music," why performance related injuries are so difficult to understand and treat. In addition to them being "multi-dimensional", they are not only influenced by "music-related variables", but also "a myriad of social, environmental, and cultural factors" (142). My case for injury is a perfect example of what this means. In addition to a lack of technical knowledge, I grew up in a small community that stressed individual talent. This psychological aspect led me to assume that my playing was naturally correct. I also grew up on a farm, where hard work was the answer to every problem. We never took thought to how we shoveled manure, lifted bales or rode horses. This not only built up tension in my body which was then carried over into my practicing each day, but it also gave me a mindset to work harder instead of smarter when pain got in my way. Social pressures of everyday posture presented slouching as ok, something I soon learned contributed to tension in my shoulders. It took both my and my professor's awareness of how these influences altered my playing for me to take the proper steps to recovery.

One of the primary misunderstandings that all musicians face is exactly what I believed: the false assumption that playing instruments or singing is something that comes naturally. The truth is, there is nothing natural about it, says Chesky. Yes, there are some who seem to pick up on rhythm or pitches more quickly than others, but the physical actions we use to play instruments or sing correctly are not something anyone's body is born knowing how to do. In fact, it takes detailed work to train such muscles that would normally develop differently when involved in different activities (142). Janet Horvath, a performing cellist and award winning author in this area of research, explains that because the focus of music is placed on the end goal, musicians become very disembodied while playing. This leads them to concentrate solely on the body parts directly involved with creating the sound instead of ensuring that their entire body is being used correctly (102). This demonstrates the psychological aspect of playing that I was taught to evaluate with the Alexander Technique.

But there is an equally important physiological aspect that connects to proper technique. Professional musicians like Horvath, as well as doctors and physicians that are aware of musicians' unique work, often refer to musicians as athletes on a small scale. This is a very accurate comparison, but how often do you see musicians doing stretches and detailed warm ups before practicing, or see trainers sitting next to them, ensuring their every movement is healthy (878)? I certainly was never warned about the importance of specific, effective warm ups before playing. In addition to this, these injuries are significantly harder to detect than the average sports injury because of the small, internal muscles, joints and ligaments involved (879). A thorough knowledge of the anatomy and physiology of the body is central for understanding how to operate or teach an instrument.

Unfortunately, according to Horvath, music education students do not receive instruction on human physiology or detailed pedagogy specific to each instrument because of the heavy workload already placed on them. But simply knowing the basics of how to play each instrument is not sufficient to demonstrate to younger students exactly what they should and should not be doing on their instruments (104). Most often school is the only musical exposure for students, so the amount of pedagogical training they receive is limited. But proper technique must be taught from the start to keep bad habits, such as crooked wrists or raised shoulders, from turning into major injuries (Palac 880). So where can we turn? Fortunately, several programs that have been formed over the past decades address this problem.

Performing Arts Medicine, a newly developed area of research in the field of science and medicine, has been working hard on making accessible, specified treatment for injured musicians around the globe. Over the years it has grown significantly, comprising of several foundations that work to boost awareness of performance-related injuries (Performing Arts Medicine). This system was formed around the 1950's as the knowledge of performance-related injuries widened and their serious threat to musicians became accepted as truth. In response to this, statements were made by school associations concerning the need for professionals in schools to prevent these injuries. But it was not until 2004 when serious action was taken in a conference held by HPSM, together with the ICSOM and PAMA. Here, matters of pedagogy and technique, as well as causes and recovery methods for the most common injuries were carefully defined. A plan of action was also outlined for how this information could be delivered to the schools and health care professionals (Palac 880).

Out of this came the introduction of physiotherapists, health care providers under the specific training of performance-related injuries. Since this level of specified care is not available from mainstream doctors and specialists, having physiotherapists to understand the specific causes and treatment has proved to be the most effective solution for injured musicians. Dr. Jan Dommerholt, an accomplished physical therapist and expert in the treatment of various pain syndromes, is an example of such a physician. As do all physiotherapists, he understands that matters beyond what can be seen on the outside is one of the biggest steps toward prevention and recovery. Asking the necessary questions such as the patient's overall musical background, type of instrument, repertoire and practice habits enable physiotherapists to implement technical strategies for each patient according to his/her situation (128). Horvath, as a professional musician herself, points out the hope of every musician: that the more this type of work becomes available, the more doctors will become informed of what action needs to be taken for injured musicians (105).

Physiotherapists also make strides in implementing prevention programs in the educational system. A recent self-awareness program, conducted in 2010 by musical health associations at a Norwegian Conservatory, led to reduce injuries by 45% after just four months (Dommerholt 128). These results reinforce the necessity of a well-rounded assessment of all areas in a musician's life. Chesky states the following in the introduction to the conference held in 2004, ' 'Educating college music students about health issues is a daunting task that requires involvement from several disciplines and perspectives. Success will depend on our ability to create and sustain working collaborations that help challenge, redefine, and expand what is currently known and accepted" (881). This is the progress being made by physiotherapists and foundations such as PAMA and HPSM and the prevention programs they implement.

As a piano performance major at Grand Valley, I have been working through my injuries for a year. It takes daily consciousness of how my entire body is correlating, and frequent assessment of pain in my muscles and joints. I am still learning more ways to release tension, but every day it gets easier, and I've grown to appreciate how complex the human body, the master of instruments, really is. Thanks to a well-acknowledged piano professor and information online, I am on a straight path to recovery and now play for several hours every day. But the battle is not over for either me or other musicians. Although many are working hard for more answers and flooding the educational system with knowledge to create safer playing environments, the gap between doctors and musicians still exists. It will take dedication on everyone's part to continue spreading awareness so the future of the performing arts can thrive, unthreatened by pain.

Word Count: 3149

Works Cited

Chesky, Chris S., et al. "Health Promotion in Schools of Music: Initial Recommendations for Schools of Music." *Medical Problems of Performing Artists*. Vol. 21, no. 3, Sept 2006, pp.142-144, hpsm.unt.edu/.

Dommerholt, Jan. "Performing Arts Medicine-Instrumentalist Musicians: Part III - Case Histories." *ScienceDirect*. Vol. 14, 2010, pp. 127-138. *ResearchGate*, 10.1016/j.jbmt.2009.02.005.

Harvath, Janet, et al. "An Orchestra Musician's Perspective on 20 Years of Performing arts Medicine." *Medical Problems of Performing Artists*. Vol. 16, no. 3, Sept. 2001, pp. 102-108. *Health Reference Center Academic*, go.galegroup.com.ezproxy.gvsu.edu/ps/i.do?p=HRCA&sw=w&u=lom_gvalleysu&v-2.1&it=r&id=GALE%7CA173187299&asid=cce1af26cba851428acb684a22daecf6.

Kok, Laura M. "Musicians' Illness Perceptions of Musculoskeletal Complaints." *Clinical Rheumatology*. Vol. 32, 2013, pp. 487-492. *PubMed*,10.1007/s10067-013-2199-1.

Palac, Judith A., and David N Grimshaw. "Music Education and Performing Arts Medicine: The State of Alliance." *Physical Medicine and Rehabilitation Clinics of North America*, Vol. 17, no.4, Nov. 2006, pp. 877-891. *PubMed*, 10.1016/j.pmr.2006.07.001.

Performing Arts Medicine Association. *Performing Arts Medicine Association: Dedicated to the Health of Performing Artists*. 2015, www.artsmed.org/about.

Toledo, Santiago D., et al. "Sports and Performing Arts Medicine. 5 Issues Relating to Musicians." *The American Academy of Physical Medicine and Rehabilitation*. Vol. 85, no. 3, 2004, pp. S72-74. *ProQuest*, dx.doi.org/10.1053/j.apmr.2003.12.006.

Trollinger, Valerie. "Performing Arts Medicine and Music Education: What Do We Really Need to Know?" *Music Educators Journal*. Vol. 92, no. 3, Nov. 2005, pp. 42-48. *ResearchGate*, 10.2307/3400196.

PORTFOLIO THREE

BY COLE HOWE

As a student in WRT 150, mechanical engineering major Cole Howe found himself in a situation many students experience in the class: about halfway through the semester, Cole realized he didn't like the topics for two of his papers. He explains, "After writing a couple of poor drafts on topics I wasn't passionate about, I realized if I didn't care about the topics, it became evident in my writing." After consulting with his instructor, Professor Joe Ketchum, and developing a plan to make sure he could meet his instructor's deadlines and requirements, Cole switched gears and focused on topics he cared about: ways to support people who, as he says, "are in tough situations in the world." This led him to explore how campaign finance laws have influenced the American political system in "America the Oligarchy," and research the impact of global warming on human health in "How the Climate Changes You."

For Cole, the most difficult essay to write was his narrative, "Running from Trouble." The essay reflects on a time when Cole made decisions he wasn't proud of, and he found it challenging to "push through the tough emotions" that came up as he recalled that period of his life as he tried to find ways to "transfer those emotions onto paper." The editors were impressed by Cole's portfolio because he was able to turn a critical eye to national and global issues, but he was willing to examine critically his own decisions as well.

Cole's Advice for WRT 150 Students

Spend time finding topics that you have passion for, write a strong outline for each essay, utilize the writing center and those around you, and start early. You might start slow or even restart, but that's okay. As long as you choose topics that you are truly interested in and work hard you're bound to do well.

RUNNING FROM TROUBLE

I had my life ahead of me and my character and personality forming faster than they ever have before. Beginning adolescence and heading into my last year of middle school, I was quite an impressionable kid, so hanging around my four closest friends was a formula for trouble. Sam, Caleb, Ricky, and Connor were the group of guys who were considered by our peers to be goofballs. They were the kids who walked the tightrope of fun every day trying to give just enough effort to get by, whilst having as much fun as they could squeeze out of every day. I was just like them. Our impulse to cause trouble and get our hearts racing, however, got us into trouble more often than intended. Early in our seventh grade year we schemed up a plan to barricade Caleb's neighborhood with trashcans, trampolines, and flowerpots, so we could watch the attempt to navigate their way out of the neighborhood like mice in a maze. This was our best scheme to date, and it even got a mention in one of the local newspapers calling that neighborhood in our home town, "the ghetto of Coopersville."

The majority of the time, our well intended mischief worked out well for us. We were always having a blast with life, and continuing to do well in everything that mattered to us. Lately, however, I was on bad terms with my family. From seventh to eighth grade, I had been grounded for about nine months, and I was currently grounded from the maze scheme since one of the neighborhood watch parents recognized me and notified the police. These groundings came in one to three month intervals, which successively got longer, and also depended on the severity of my actions and whether or not the police had been involved. The root cause for my punishments virtually always came from the shenanigans I pulled with my buddies.

Fourth of July weekend, before heading into eighth grade, I went camping with my family in Pentwater. Due to my annoyance of always being grounded, I planned to stay out of trouble this time. As I had gone camping in the past, my family would always allow me to bring a few friends. After I pleaded to my parents that we would keep our noses clean, somehow, even after my atrocious year of actions, my parents approved of me bringing the gang with us.

Contributed by Cole Howe. Copyright ©Kendall Hunt Publishing Company.

They even told me that we were able to sleep in a tent outside of our camper, come to find out, this was only because there wasn't enough room for the five of us boys inside. I knew they would be very annoyed with us boisterous teenagers anyway. There was one condition though: If I got into trouble, again, during this trip I would be grounded for six months. Half a year was the longest proposed grounding time I have ever heard from them. They weren't bluffing either. When they found out that Ricky and I had been the ones throwing firecrackers at our awful instructor Mrs. Parson's house at night, they kept their word with grounding me for three months. Although I had an extreme urge to goof off with the guys, I had to suppress it because I was not willing to do this time stuck in my room day after day.

On the morning of July third, before heading up to Pentwater on the trip, I requested to my friends that we must stay out of trouble this weekend. After an attempt of persuasion to just be more careful, they complied. The next afternoon we arrived at the campsite and we were ecstatic. The weather predictions for the weekend were amazing, our campsite was right beside the beach, we were only a short walk from downtown Pentwater, and there were other teenagers to meet everywhere in sight. For the next few hours, we set up our tent, enjoyed a meal with my family, and laid out in the sun. As the sun beat down on us, our fresh sunburns convinced us to leave the beach. We all agreed to change out of our swimsuits, grab some cash, and head towards town to check out the stores. In town, there was more than we expected. We passed through candy stores, clothing stores, ice cream parlors, and finally made our way to an old general store. The inside of the store was cluttered with a variety of interesting cheap items. We fanned out and browsed the store aisles until I heard Caleb turn and yell, "Guys look, fireworks!" We all stopped and rushed over to where he was standing. In front of him were three enormous pyramids of fireworks on a dark wooden table.

The table seemed to have every type of firework that was listed off in the firework stand scene from the movie *Joe Dirt*. We sifted through the explosives to find the loudest and brightest ones. To our delight the fireworks were cheap enough for us to fill our pockets full. After putting our money together, we realized we also had enough cash to fill up the front of Caleb's shirt as he stretched it out in front of him and pulled it up to make a big shirt bucket. While heading to the checkout table, I paused and said with a sense of disappointment, "Wait guys, aren't these fireworks illegal for us?" All of our smiles dropped and we turned around to put the fireworks back from where they came from.

Behind the counter, a man with white hair and a balding head said, "The new law in Michigan states that anyone over the age of eighteen can buy fireworks. It'd only be illegal if you were all underage."

We stood still and gave blank stares to the cashier, then Sam abruptly yelled out, "I'm eighteen!" Knowing that none of us were a day over sixteen, Sam, the youngest of all of us, didn't even have a few chin hairs to display. He was certainly the worst one of us to proclaim that he was an adult. I decided that attempting to buy the fireworks illegally wouldn't hurt, so I turned back towards the counter once again, set my fireworks in front of Sam, and the others followed my lead. The clerk looked Sam up and down, and before any transactions, he asked to see his ID. We looked towards Sam in a moment of suspense, hoping he could save us. Sam peered into the cashier's eyes and replied boldly, "I never carry it with me." The clerk proceeded to ask Sam for his date of birth, to which Sam, without hesitation, uttered, "April 2, 1995, and lemme' get a couple lighters too." To our astonishment, the clerk smirked at us, rang up the fireworks, and put them in a hefty brown paper bag.

"Have a nice day, boys." he said. We left the store quietly, but I felt as if my pounding heart could be heard for a mile. We knew he let us off the hook. Besides our subtle differences, all of us had the same baby face and the acne of a typical middle schooler. I checked my phone and saw that it was almost 7:00 P.M. We decided to head back to my camper to settle our rumbling stomachs and fuel up for a venture on "Mt. Old Baldy," the 1470 foot sand dune within the Pentwater campground (Summit Post).

By sundown, we headed to Mt. Old Baldy with a curfew of 11:00 P.M. We hiked the dirt trails through the forest along the side to reach the summit. Upon arrival, we found that no other adventurers were around. We scoured the area to find an open spot in the sand where we could all sit together, then took out a few of the "screamers" from the bag of fireworks. We used teamwork as Caleb held his hands around the lighter to block the light wind as I lit the wick to the firework that Connor held. With a trail of black smoke, sparks, and the sound of a screeching eagle, the screamer shot off like a rocket. After a few seconds of rapid ascension, the firework blew up making the sound of a gunshot and giving off a bright flash that illuminated the night sky. The adrenaline rush from the presence of danger and the exciting explosion encouraged us to light even more.

Over the course of an hour, we dug to the bottom of the bag and lit all of the fireworks we had. We rushed to use them all because 11:00 P.M. was creeping up quickly. By the end of our self performed show, each of us had burnt and black spotted hands from taking turns holding the wicks while the others lit them. The air was filled with smoke and the smell of gunpowder lingered to our noses. I checked my watch and saw that it was already 10:45 P.M. I turned to the guys and said, "Alright boys, our work here is finished. It's time for us to head back." Since it was such a good night, they were satisfied to leave on schedule.

We closely followed the dirt trail off the side of Mt. Old Baldy to get back. It was difficult to retrace our steps back to the campsite though because the sun had set over an hour ago. Without the flashlights from our phones, we were isolated in darkness. Along the way we talked about which fireworks were our favorites and which ones to get next time. We all agreed that we needed to get more because the rush from them was so much fun. With only a little difficulty, we made the majority of the trip back and we rounded the last corner of the trail. Suddenly, two bright flashlights beamed at us through the trees and we heard a man yell in a deep coarse voice, "DNR, freeze!" We froze under the lights. The thought of how my parents would react when the DNR brought me back made a lump form in my throat. The two officers who began in pursuit from thirty yards away were now only a few steps away from getting us.

We knew we were in for an earful and a bad trip if we got caught. Without speaking to one another, we clicked off our flashlights and dashed back up the trail. Racing up the hill in the light would have been hard, but running at full speed from DNR officers when you can't see your hand in front of your own face doesn't compare. The tradeoff for not having our flashlights on came every few seconds when I would run into logs and bushes. My only cue as to where my friends were was the sounds of their heavy breathing. I soon realized that I had lost three of them already. Miraculously, I made it to the top of the hill. Despite my efforts, two more flashlights beamed into my face and a DNR officer grabbed my arm. I had been caught. Ricky came up the hill right behind me. As the second officer tried to grab Ricky, he used his superior quickness to juke the officer out and run down the face of the dune. The officer who was holding me by the arm saw this and yelled, "Grab him!" to the officer left in the dust, and dropped my arm from his grip.

Seeing another opportunity to get away, as soon as he let me go I jumped feet first off of the far side of Mt. Old Baldy. I hadn't realized how steep the hill was until I began tumbling uncontrollably down the side. I couldn't help myself from cutting my legs up from loose branches and hitting tree trunks. After rolling for a bit, I finally made it to the bottom of Mt. Old Baldy, and I began to run the outskirts of the campground back to the tent we were staying in. I hoped the others would be smart enough to realize this was our safe spot.

After circling the entire premises of the campground, I got close enough to my tent where I felt I could make a break for it. I sprinted through the cold sand attempting to stay out of sight as much as possible, and grabbed the zipper. I unzipped the tent door and crawled inside to find that Caleb and Ricky had beaten me there. Within another few minutes, Connor came back to the tent breathing hard. Even though we had ran from authoritiy together before, we were all still amazed that none of us had been caught, in the face of four DNR officers attempting to trap us from both exits of the dune. We rejoiced together, knowing that Sam would be back soon to join us, and each of us eagerly shared our route to freedom.

After a half an hour had passed, we began to worry. I stuck my head out of the tent and scanned the area before deciding to greet my parents inside the camper. Although I broke curfew by nearly twenty minutes, they were in a good mood, so once again, I was off the hook. I came back to the tent, and as another ten minutes passed we finally found Sam. Slowly unzipping the tent door, we looked out to find Sam accompanied by two of the DNR officers standing behind him. They asked us to come out from the tent, and after all crawling out they began to bombard us with questions. Why were we up there past campsite hours? Why did we run? Did we understand the risk of wildfires due to fireworks in that area? We answered each of their questions politely and honestly. After the lectures and making sure we knew our actions were wrong, the officers told us we weren't in any trouble. All they asked of us was to learn from this experience and not do it again. We quickly wrapped up our conversation with them, and they told us to have a good night.

As we walked back to our tent we quietly scolded Sam with our eyes for being caught while waiting to make sure the officers were out of sight. After half a minute had passed, I checked to see if the coast was clear, and we all began to laugh about the situation and bash on Sam for being the one to get caught. Connor told us he jumped off of the back of Mt. Old Baldy and hid behind a tree, Ricky and Caleb met at the front of Mt. Old Baldy and hid in the campground bathrooms together, I fell off the side and ran around the campground, and Sam, being the dunce he was, hid under a picnic table and got caught. Besides for Sam's stupid decisions though, we were all dumbfounded with how lucky we had gotten. How could we have done all of those wrongdoings and not gotten into any legal trouble, let alone not have had my parents find out? Knowing we were pushing our luck to the brink, we decided to call it a night.

In the morning we went about our business as usual. None of us spoke more than a few words during breakfast, and I was quick to get my friends and myself away from my parents, knowing the risk that one of them might spill the beans about the night before. Deciding that our new sunburns weren't too bad, we went back to the beach to swim in the water all day. We had so much fun playing football in the water, tubing behind our parents' friend's boat, and soaking up the sun again that we forgot all about our worries from the night before. But we were reminded much faster than I thought we would be. As we came back to my campsite, my heart dropped into my stomach as I saw my parents speaking with the two DNR officers who brought Sam back to us. As I walked closer my parents called me over to speak with them.

My mother said to me, "Cole, these two nice officers told us what you and your friends did last night." Immediately, I registered that I had been bamboozled by the DNR officers on our first meeting. I thought, 'Maybe they were going to give me a criminal record.' Tears began to fill my eyes as I thought more and realized all of the possible consequences for what I had done. My stream of thought was interrupted by my mother again. "Luckily, they aren't pressing any charges, but they are happy to hear that we are taking matters into our own hands. You are grounded for six months. No cellphone, no Xbox, no going out. All of your fun is over. I hope you're happy."

Although I was extremely disappointed and cried then, today, however, I am happy. With the years of peer pressure filled high school imminent, my teachings from my parents paid off as I repeatedly had the self discipline to stand up for myself when faced with situations involving theft, drugs, and alcohol when I didn't want to take part. For some people, having foresight for actions seems to be an easy thing, but I needed many severe repercussions to shape my decision making. I honestly believe that if I hadn't been punished each and every one of those times I had done something incredibly stupid, I wouldn't be in the spot I am today. If I hadn't had the same friends pushing me to do idiotic things early in life, I wouldn't have the knowledge of what to look out for if a group similar to mine peer pressured me today. I might not be sitting in this chair writing this essay, but instead be in a jail because two officers weren't satisfied with my parents taking matters into their own hands. So for all of the early life mistakes, the poor habits, the long groundings, and the angry lectures from my parents, I am thankful.

Word Count: 3026

Works Cited

"Michigan County Highpoints." *Summit Post*, 13 July 2011, http://www.summitpost.org/michigan-county-highpoints/369617.

AMERICA THE OLIGARCHY

On January 21, 2010, American politics took a nosedive into the pool of corruption. This day was not on a presidential or midterm election, but it was the date that the Supreme Court, in a 5-to-4 ruling, invalidated two provisions of the Federal Election Campaign Act (FECA) within the case Citizens United v. FEC. This case "struck down the longstanding prohibition on corporations from using their general treasury funds to make independent expenditures," and "determined that these prohibitions constitute a 'ban on speech' in violation of the First Amendment" (Whitaker 141). This led the Supreme Court to rule that "Spending is speech, and is therefore protected by the Constitution - even if the speaker is a corporation" (Dunbar). This means that corporations themselves, not the citizens that compose them, may spend unlimited amounts of money on political actions, and restricting corporations to do so is a violation of the First Amendment. As proven since, giving this large shift of power to corporations has led to a great deal of trouble. The Supreme Court case Citizens United v. FEC should be overturned because it leads to Congress working against their constituents' interests, the American people disagree with the decision made, and because there are more effective campaign finance systems.

Before the decision of Citizens United v. FEC, the two main ways to support political candidates were through candidate committees and political action committees, also known as PACs. Every politician running for Congress was permitted to have a candidate committee, and PACs could support those committees, but contributions directly from corporations, labor unions, and foreign nationals were banned. The limit for these candidate committees was only $2,700 per election to keep unreasonable spending in check (Kreig). Since the ruling of Citizens United v. FEC, however, steps have been taken to use immense sums of money for political purposes. One of the ways in which corporations and individuals have done so is through what are called "super PACs." A super PAC is like a traditional PAC or candidate committee, but they are allowed to accept unlimited amounts of contributions from corporations, labor unions, and individuals. Although super PACs are prohibited from communicating directly to candidates, they can spend unlimited amounts for political reasons (Kreig). This is usually done through advertising in favor or against certain political candidates. This change in policy has led to overwhelming changes in campaign outcomes by using extreme sums of money to buy candidates a better chance to win.

Initially, the allowance of infinite sums of money for political purposes may seem unimportant, but the issues become evident when observing a typical campaign cycle. Beginning with their first days in office, "your newly elected Congressional representative is expected to spend half of his or her working hours dialing for dollars at a secret phone bank near Capitol Hill" (Selleck). Knowing that any voter's representatives are spending half of their time calling donors for money rather than working to benefit their constituents should infuriate a voter, but it gets worse. When looking into the actions of the elected, analysis confirms that "the more time lawmakers spend fundraising, the greater the influence of contributions in their chambers. That is, the more members engage in either type of fundraising, the more they, and consequently their chambers, prioritize the interests of donors" (Powell). So not only are Congressional officials spending half of their time not working for their constituents, but they are potentially spending half of their time working for their donors which sometimes goes directly against what their constituents value most.

So why are virtually all Congressmen doing this? When looking at the statistics, the modern campaign financing system practically forces them to. United Republic, a nonpartisan nonprofit, found that 91% of the time the higher-spending candidate won their race in an analysis of the 2012 congressional races (Lowery). Without the sufficient funds to help candidates with transportation, advertisements, and pay for their campaign teams, they are given extremely unlikely odds to compete in their respective races. So how much money are they really raising? The same analysis found that the winning candidates spent on average $2.3 million on their races. This amount of money to run for just one seat in office is also nearly impossible to reach without the current fundraising methods.

These current fundraising methods, however, lead to many head-scratching outcomes in American politics. A poll from Quinnipiac University in June 2017, found that 94% of Americans support requiring background checks for all gun buyers (Kertscher). Despite the overwhelming support from the American people, legislation requiring companies selling arms to do background checks on the buyers continues to be voted against in Congress. Although there is not a certain cause of why this happens, many people point fingers at the National Rifle Association (NRA). In 2012, the NRA spent $19.7 million on candidates who tweeted "thoughts and prayers" in wake of the San Bernardino shooting (Geier). This, of course, comes with the representatives actively pushing against legislation that works toward stopping mass shootings from happening again. This case of Congress not representing their constituents' views, however, is not an outlier. The non representation from Congress in these instances is frustrating to voters, and it is evident in the congressional approval rating of 16% for September of 2017 (Swift).

With the realization of how important donations are to candidates, one may argue that the American people should simply donate more, so Congress will be able to represent the people instead of just their top donors. This seems to be a completely reasonable counterpoint, but the argument falls short because it fails to address wealth inequality in America. Large corporations are able to donate top dollar to candidates, but sadly, the average American can not. In an analysis from the Social Security Administration on November 7th, 2016, it was found that "50 percent of wage earners had net compensation less than or equal to the median wage, which is estimated to be $30,557.71 for 2016" (SSA). That salary is just above the federal poverty level for a family of four for 2017 at $28,290 (HHS). This knowledge on the average American's financial status displays that the typical American worker is not always fortunate enough to spend their hard earned dollars to be represented, but is using that money to support themselves and/or their family.

Nevertheless, the American people are not ignorant on the issue of money corruption in politics. In a poll titled "Americans' Views on Money in Politics" by *The New York Times* and CBS from 2015, 1,022 adults were asked for their views on money in politics. Regardless of their political affiliation, Americans seemed to agree on these issues. When asked, "Thinking about the role of money in American political campaigns today, do you think money has too much influence, too little influence or is it about right?" 84% of them answered that it has too much of an influence ("Americans' Views"). When asked whether the American political funding system needs changes, 85% of them answered within the categories of either it needing "fundamental changes" or that it needs to be "completely rebuilt" (Americans' Views). In a question directly connected to the Citizens United v. FEC case, when asked, "Currently, groups not affiliated with a candidate are able to spend unlimited amounts on advertisements during a political campaign. Do you think this kind of spending should be limited by law, or should it remain unlimited?" 78% of responders answered "should be limited" ("Americans' Views"). These results display that the high majority of American citizens disagree with the ruling that the Supreme Court has made in the case.

As money has been heavily influencing modern American politics this may lead one to argue that publicly funded and super PAC free elections are simply not possible in America. To prove this wrong, one can look no further than some of America's own states. In the United States for the 2015-2016 election cycle, thirteen states already have some form of publicly funded elections. In three of these states (Arizona, Connecticut, and Maine), they offer clean election programs. In these programs "candidates are encouraged to collect small contributions (no more than $5) from a number of individuals (depending on the position sought) to demonstrate that he or she has enough public support to warrant public funding of his or her campaign. In return, the commission established for the program gives the candidate a sum of money equal to the expenditure limit set for the election" ("State Public Financing"). This form of publicly financing campaigns is favored by those states' citizens rather than our current national system, and it avoids a cash grab for politicians due to there being expenditure limits for campaigns (Cruikshank).

Although publicly financed elections are within only some American states today, shifting to publicly financed elections on a national scale is possible and may not be as daunting of a task as one might believe. In many countries around the world including: France, Germany, Canada, and Norway, they all have some form of publicly funded elections (Thompson). In France, campaign expenditures and donations are capped, and all forms of paid advertisements are prohibited 3 months prior to the elections, but instead political advertisements are aired free of charge and on an equal basis (Library of Congress). In Norway in 2017, 74.7% of all funding of political parties came from government subsidies on an equal basis due to popularity, and only 7.9% came from contributions from private interests ("Political parties' financing").

To compare this to the United States, the FEC estimates that 7 billion dollars was spent in the 2012 election year alone and that 3.2 billion was spent by candidates (Parti). This means that the other 3.8 billion spent, which accounts for 54.2% of the total spending, was from outside sources such as PACs and super PACs. This spending went up over $697 million since its previous election years of 2008 (Prokop). In between this time the Citizens United v. FEC ruling happened.

With 7 billion dollars being spent in federal elections in 2012, opposers of this issue might argue that having alternative routes to financing might cause the citizens to foot this enormous bill which would raise taxes. However, when looking deeper into this issue, one can find that there are many systems that would be imperceptible to the average American's taxes while also being more effective in disarming the extremely influential individuals and corporations than our current system. One option is by passing the Government By the People Act of 2015 which "[gives] every citizen a voucher worth up to $50 through a 'My Voice Tax Credit' for campaign contributions in $5 increments, and it would aim to make small donations as influential as large donations by matching any donation on a six-to-one level through the establishment of a Freedom From Influence Fund" ("H.R. 20"). Another option would be to pass the Fair Elections Now Act which would "also allow candidates to raise unlimited donations so long as they did not individually exceed $150." ("S. 1538"). Both of these bills would "level the playing field for candidates who can demonstrate a minimum level of support while also helping to free up incumbent members of Congress from the burden of spending hours each day dialing for dollars rather than working on legislation or helping their constituents." (Berman). In these systems the heavy influence from big money interests would be diminished and citizens would not have to spend large sums of money.

Regardless of political ideology this is an issue that the majority of Americans can agree on. Although the United States' chaotic system continues to move in the wrong direction on policy, frustrated individuals tired of establishment politics are not at square one on reversing this issue. Wolf PAC, a group whose sole purpose is to "get an amendment to the U.S. Constitution that will reverse the damage that has been done by the U.S. Supreme Court around campaign finance reform" is one of many organizations who work towards changing the system (Hartson). Even without joining a group like Wolf PAC, simply recognizing of the amount of private money that candidates running for office are taking and knowing where that money is coming from is helpful to keep in mind while voting. Acts such as spreading awareness of this issue and pushing your representatives to make a policy change can help lead a revolution towards a true democracy where the people are represented, not just the ones with the deepest pockets. For today, we are left to deal with as Mark Twain once said, "the best Congress that money can buy." ("Mark Twain").

Word Count: 2103

Works Cited

"Americans' Views on Money in Politics." *The New York Times*, 2 June 2015, https://www.nytimes.com/interactive/2015/06/02/us/politics/money-in-politics-poll.html

Berman, Russell. "How Can the U.S. Shrink the Influence of Money in Politics?" *The Atlantic*, 16 Mar. 2016, https://www.theatlantic.com/politics/archive/2016/03/fix-money-in-politics/473214/

Cruikshank, Brain. "Overview of State Laws on Public Financing." *National Conference of State Legislatures*, http://www.ncsl.org/research/elections-and-campaigns/public-financing-of-campaigns-overview.aspx. Accessed 30 Oct. 2017.

Dunbar, John. "The 'Citizens United' Decision and Why it Matters." *The Center for Public Integrity*, 14 Mar. 2016. https://www.publicintegrity.org/2012/10/18/11527/citizens-united-decision-and-why-it-matters

Geier, Ben. "NRA's Massive Political Spending Gains Attention." *Fortune*, 3 Dec. 2015, http://fortune.com/2015/12/03/san-bernadino-nra-political-spending-gun-violence/

Hartson, Alison. "The Logical Path to End Corruption." *Medium.com*, 20 Apr. 2017, https://medium.com/wolf-pac/the-logical-path-to-end-corruption-a64c1d06394b

"H.R. 20 (114th): Government By the People Act of 2015." *GovTrack*, 13 Apr. 2016, https://www.govtrack.us/congress/bills/114/hr20/summary

Kertscher, Tom. "Do 90% of Americans Support Background Checks for All Gun Sales." *Politifact*, 3 Oct. 2017, http://www.politifact.com/wisconsin/statements/2017/oct/03/chris-abele/do-90-americans-support-background-checks-all-gun-/

Kreig, Gregory J. "What Is a Super PAC? A Short History." *ABC News*, 9 Aug. 2012, http://abcnews.go.com/Politics/OTUS/super-pac-short-history/story?id=16960267

"Mark Twain: Best Government You Can Buy." *Made of Money*, 6 Dec. 2014, http://itsamoneything.com/money/mark-twain-best-government-buy/#.WhISwUqnHIU

Lowery, Wesley. "91% of the Time the Better-Financed Candidate wins. Don't Act Surprised." *Washington Post*, 4 Apr. 2014. https://www.washingtonpost.com/news/the-fix/wp/2014/04/04/think-money-doesnt-matter-in-elections-this-chart-says-youre-wrong/?utm_term=.40c4a1d0dfb2

Parti, Tarini. "FEC: $7B Spent on 2012 Campaign." *Politico*. 31 Jan. 2013, https://www.politico.com/story/2013/01/7-billion-spent-on-2012-campaign-fec-says-087051

"Political Parties' Fnancing." *Statistics Norway*, 4 Sep. 2017, http://www.ssb.no/en/partifin

Powell, Lynda. "How money talks in state legislatures." *Washington Post*, 5 Nov. 2013, https://www.washingtonpost.com/news/monkey-cage/wp/2013/11/05/the-influence-of-money-in-u-s-politics/?utm_term=.9f741be21452

Prokop, Andrew. "40 charts that explain money in politics." *Vox*, 30 July 2014, https://www.vox.com/2014/7/30/5949581/money-in-politics-charts-explain

Selleck, Stacey. "Congress Spends More Time Dialing For Dollars Than On Legislative Work." *Termlimits.com*, 26 Apr. 2016, https://www.termlimits.com/congress-fundraising-priority/

"S. 1538 (114th): Fair Elections Now Act." *GovTrack*, 10 June 2015, https://www.govtrack.us/congress/bills/114/s1538

"State Public Financing Options 2015-2016 Election Cycle." *National Conference of State Legislatures*, http://www.ncsl.org/Portals/1/documents/legismgt/elect/StatePublicFinancingOptionsChart2015.pdf. Accessed 30 Oct. 2017.

Swift, Art. "Congress Approval Remains at 16% in September." *Gallup News*, 13 Sep. 2017, http://news.gallup.com/poll/218984/congress-approval-remains-september.aspx

Thompson, Nick. "International campaign finance: How do other countries compare?" *CNN*, 5 Mar. 2012, http://www.cnn.com/2012/01/24/world/global-campaign-finance/index.html

United States. Dept. of Health & Human Services (HHS). *Poverty Guidelines*, 31 Jan. 2017.

United States. Library of Congress. Campaign Finance: France, 1 July 2017. Web.

United States. Social Security Administration (SSA). Wage Statistics for 2016, 13 Nov. 2017.

Whitaker, Paige L. *The First Amendment: Select Issues*. Nova Science Publishers, 2010.

HOW THE CLIMATE CHANGES YOU

In modern day America the debate on whether climate change is actually happening often seems to be in dead heat. A poll from Gallup in March of 2017 found that 50% of Americans are categorized as "concerned believers," when asked their opinion on a series of statements regarding climate change (Saad). This record high rate of individuals believing climate change is a concern looks as if it will continue its upward trend as the word continues to spread that "multiple studies published in peer-reviewed scientific journals show that 97 percent or more of actively publishing climate scientists agree: Climate-warming trends over the past century are extremely likely due to human activities" (Scientific Consensus). Since the scientific community is at a virtual consensus on the issue, the notion that climate change is not happening may be dismissed. This fact, however, may be hard to swallow since it leads one to the realization that its effects are also happening. Not only are the effects on the environment happening, but there is a less talked about effect: human health. Analyzing the data on climate change may lead one to be weary about the impacts on humanity's welfare due to temperature related, air quality, and extreme weather effects.

When based off of the 1951-1980 average global temperatures, the 2016 temperature deviation is 0.99 degrees Celsius (1.782 degrees Fahrenheit) above the average over that period. As shown in Figure 1 on the following page, "sixteen of the 17 warmest years in the 136-year record all have occurred since 2001, with the exception of 1998" and, "the year 2016 ranks as the warmest on record" ("Global"). These facts are not simply a fluke due to random chance, but instead from what climate scientists call the "greenhouse effect." The greenhouse effect works like this: "First, sunlight shines onto the Earth's surface, where it is absorbed and then radiates back into the atmosphere as heat. In the atmosphere, 'greenhouse' gases trap some of this heat, and the rest escapes into space. The more greenhouse gases are in the atmosphere, the more heat gets trapped" ("What"). This effect is happening at such an unusual rate due to the levels of "greenhouse gases" we have in the global atmosphere currently, which are higher than the last 650,000 years ("What").

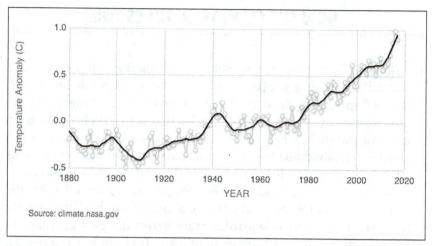

Source: climate.nasa.gov

Figure 1   The temperature deviation in degrees Celsius from 1880 to 2017 ("Global").

The effects from increased global temperatures over the past few decades are having not only an effect on the global environment, but on human health as well. For many places around the world where high temperatures do not typically cause health problems, the effects of global rising temperatures often goes unnoticed. In places where it often does cause health problems, however, the recent surge in global temperatures often pushes these regions' temperatures over a tipping point that makes these health concerns deadly. In coming decades, "U.N. officials and climate scientists predict that the mushrooming populations of the Middle East and North Africa will face extreme water scarcity, temperatures almost too hot for human survival and other consequences of global warming" (Naylor). In July of 2016, Basra, Iraq, recorded a land temperature of 129 degrees Fahrenheit and Mitribah, Kuwait reached a temperature of 129.2 degrees Fahrenheit. The World Meteorological Organization confirmed that these two temperatures were the highest ever recorded in the Eastern Hemisphere (Naylor). The recording setting temperature spikes in these areas have led climate scientists to believe that the livelihoods of the men and women inhabiting them are "potentially at risk" (Verner 13). Since the Middle Eastern and North African regions are home to about a half a billion people, many of which are too poor to afford an air conditioning unit, life may become extremely difficult. (Naylor). In the wake of the Basaran heat wave of 2016, a 26-year-old university

Classification	Heat Index	Effect on the body
Caution	80°F - 90°F	Fatigue possible with prolonged exposure and/or physical activity
Extreme Caution	90°F - 103°F	Heat stroke, heat cramps, or heat exhaustion possible with prolonged exposure and/or physical activity
Danger	103°F - 124°F	Heat cramps or heat exhaustion likely, and heat stroke possible with prolonged exposure and/or physical activity
Extreme Danger	125°F or higher	Heat stroke highly likely

Figure 2 The effects of temperatures on the human body (Romm).

student said that stepping outside is like, "walking into a fire," and, "It's like everything on your body -your skin, your eyes, your nose- starts to burn" (Naylor). Similarly, in August of 2017 temperatures once again soared above 120 degrees in a heat wave nicknamed "Lucifer." During this heat wave, birds in Kuwait were reported to have been "dropping out of the sky" (Romm). These extreme temperatures, along with humidity levels in the region, affect humans as well by "[preventing] the human body from cooling down through sweating, leading to hyperthermia" (Romm). As the National Weather Service describes in Figure 2 above, these temperatures may cause "Heat cramps or heat exhaustion" and even "heat [strokes]" (Romm).

"One in eight total global deaths" are due to the product of climate change known as "air pollution" (Nadadur 7). Air pollution is the presence of "chemicals or particles in the air that can harm the health of humans, animals, and plants" (World Health Organization or WHO). It can happen from either natural sources such as smoke from wildfires or ash from volcanoes, or it can be created through anthropogenic sources (by people) with emissions from factories, cars, planes, and aerosol cans. The majority of air pollution happens from anthropogenic sources ("Air Pollution"). Although air pollution happens essentially everywhere in the world, its effects are most common in large cities where emissions are concentrated. This overwhelmingly affects poorer regions in the world as large cities in poor and developing nations tend to have more pollution than cities in developing nations. In India, the second most populated country on the planet, nearly one and a half billion people are at severe health risks (Schultz et al.).

In 2016, the US Embassy in Delhi, India put Delhi's AQI level at 999 on the standard Air Quality Index chart (Griffiths). The AQI is an index for reporting daily air quality, and New Delhi is "reporting levels almost five times those considered 'unhealthy' by the US environmental protection agency" (Griffiths). To put this into perspective, an AQI greater than 300 would "trigger health warnings of emergency conditions" and affect "the entire population" of India. (Air Quality Index (AQI) Basics). Air pollution experts say that "prolonged exposure to such high concentrations of [this level are] equivalent to smoking more than two packs of cigarettes a day" (Kumar). Locals in the area say that the air pollution tastes smoky, irritates the throat, smells of paint, saps their strength, and leaves them nauseated like "a never-ending case of car sickness" (Kumar). These "off the standard chart levels" have forced India's government to take action. The state's chief minister, Arvind Kejriwal, said on Twitter: "Delhi has become a gas chamber..." (Kumar). After passing a school bus that had two children throwing up out of the windows, Manish Sisodia, the deputy chief minister of Delhi State ordered his officers to "close all the schools" (Schultz et al.).

As India continues its efforts to lessen the effects of air pollution on its citizens, one may still be worried about their air quality if they live in an urban area. Although the atmospheres in most urban areas are not likely to be labeled as "gas chambers," the World Health Organization reported in 2016 that "more than 80% of people living in urban areas that monitor air pollution are exposed to air quality levels that exceed WHO limits" (WHO). The World Health Organization also states that as urban air quality declines "the risk of stroke, heart disease, lung cancer, and chronic and acute respiratory diseases, including asthma, increases for the people who live in them" and that "ambient air pollution, made of high concentrations of small and fine particulate matter, is the greatest environmental risk to health—causing more than 3 million premature deaths worldwide every year" (WHO).

Another hotly debated topic over the past two decades, how climate change affects extreme weather, has led to a new field of research dubbed as "extreme event attribution." This field of study is primarily focused on exploring "[humanity's] fingerprint on extreme weather," and researchers in the field have been finding proof of it since 2000. In more than 140 studies that surveyed weather events from around the world, the results mounted evidence that "human activity is raising the risk of some types of extreme weather, especially those linked to heat" (Pearce et al.). In an analysis in 2017 from Carbon Brief, a UK-based website in the field of extreme event attribution, they wrote that "63% of all extreme weather events studied to date were made more likely or more severe by human-caused climate change. Heat waves account for nearly half of such events (46%), droughts make up 21%, and heavy rainfall or floods account for 14%" (Pearce et al.). In addition, the events are not likely to slow down as climate scientists agree "It's becoming amply clear that a warming world will, on the whole, see more extreme weather" (Plumer).

Although the link may initially seem unclear, rising global temperatures are, again, who climate scientists point fingers to as extreme weather becomes increasingly more common. The World Resources Institute shows rising global temperatures are the cause for heat waves, which in turn cause more warming. They also say that global warming leads to increased sea levels, which increases the risk of storm surges, and that warmer oceans lead to higher energy in coastal storms. The U.S. National Climate Assessment states that the "higher temperatures lead to increased rates of evaporation, leading to rapid drying of soils. This can not only contribute to drought conditions but can stoke forest fires" (Extreme Weather). These effects of climate change led many climate scientists to worry that the worst is yet to come. In the summer of 2017, the climate scientists were proved right.

In the months of July-September alone, the world faced: a 106 degree Fahrenheit heat wave in California that left six dead and thousands without power; massive floods across India, Nepal, and Bangladesh that affected 40 million and left 1,300 killed and 1.5 million homeless; Hurricane Irma that left at least 31 dead in the Northern Caribbean and Florida; Hurricane Harvey which killed at least 70 in Texas; and more than 80 wildfires in the United States which burned over 1.5 million acres in 9 states (World Resources Institute). As the world continues to give record breaking greenhouse emissions, Carbon Brief and other extreme event attribution research groups' work leads one to recognize that extreme weather events are likely to continue to become more frequent as the world warms. As the results over the past decades have shown, this is likely to lead to more deaths, power losses, and home displacements for the world as the rising global temperature trend persists.

As the effects of climate change impact the world through heat waves, air pollution, and extreme weather events leaving many in danger, world leaders have been taking steps to combat this issue. In Paris, France, on December 12, 2015, representatives from 196 nations signed the Paris Climate Accord, which aims to lessen greenhouse emissions and limit the rise of global temperatures. The central agreement of the Paris Climate Accord is laid out in one phrase: "Holding the increase in global average temperature to well below 2 degrees [Celsius] above pre-industrial levels." The Paris Climate Accord also pushes to reach many other "green agreements," but their long term goal is to push for net zero emissions by the mid-century (Domonoske). Although these worldwide changes have been put into place to slow the rate of climate changing effects, one may still wonder if enough is being done to protect humanity's health.

Word Count: 1915

Works Cited

"Air pollution." *National Geographic*, https://www.national geographic.org/encyclopedia/air-pollution/. Accessed 23 Nov. 2017.

Domonoske, Camila. "So What Exactly Is In The Paris Climate Accord?" *National Public Radio*, 1 June 2017. https://www.npr.org/sections/thetwoway/2017/06/01/531048986/so-what-exactly-is-in-the-paris-climate-accord

"Global Temperature." *NASA*, 21 Nov. 2017. https://climate.nasa.gov/vital-signs/global-temperature/

Griffiths, James. "New Delhi Is The Most Polluted City On Earth Right Now." *CNN*, 8 Nov. 2016, http://www.cnn.com/2016/11/07/asia/india-new-delhi-smog-pollution/index.html

Kumar, Hari. "Delhi, Blanketed in Toxic Haze, 'Has Become a Gas Chamber.'" *The New York Times*, 7 Nov. 2017, https://www.nytimes.com/2017/11/07/world/asia/delhi-pollution-gas-chamber.html?_r=0

Naylor, Hugh. "An Epic Middle East Heat Wave Could Be Global Warming's Hellish Curtain-Raiser." *The Washington Post*, 10 Aug. 2016, https://www.washingtonpost.com/world/middle_east/an-epic-middle-east-heat-wave-could-be-global-warmings-hellish-curtain-raiser/2016/08/09/c8c717d4-5992-11e6-8b48-0cb344221131_story.html?utm_term=.a1d4ed489b13

Nadadur, Srikanth S., and John W. Hollingsworth. *Air Pollution and Health Effects*. Humana Press, 2015.

Pearce, Rosamund, and Roz Pidcock. "Mapped: How Climate Change Affects Extreme Weather Around The World." *Carbon Brief*, 6 July 2017, https://www.carbonbrief.org/mapped-how-climate-change-affects-extreme-weather-around-the-world.

Plumer, Brad. "Global Warming Increases the Frequency and Severity of Natural Disasters." *Nature Publishing Group*, vol. 458, no. 7669, Aug. 2017, http://ic.galegroup.com/ic/ovic/ViewpointsDetailsPage/.

Romm, Joe. "New study: 'Super Heat Waves' of 131°F Coming if Global Warming Continues Unchecked." *ThinkProgress*, 14 Aug. 2017, https://thinkprogress.org/super-heatwaves-coming-study-warns-955962bd275a/

Saad, Lydia. "Half in U.S. Are Now Concerned Global Warming Believers." *Gallup News*, 27 Mar. 2017, http://news.gallup.com/poll/207119/half-concerned-global-warming-believers.aspx

Schultz, Kai, et al. "In India, Air So Dirty Your Head Hurts." *The New York Times*, 8 Nov. 2017, https://www.nytimes.com/2017/11/08/world/asia/india-air-pollution.html

"Scientific consensus: Earth's climate is warming." *NASA*, 21 Nov. 2017. https://climate.nasa.gov/scientific-consensus/

United States. Air Quality Index. Air Quality Index (AQI) Basics, 31 Aug. 2016. https://airnow.gov/index.cfm?action=aqibasics.aqi

United States. Global Change Research Program. "Extreme Weather," 2014. http://nca2014.globalchange.gov/highlights/report-findings/extreme-weather

Verner, Dorte. *Adaptation to a Changing Climate in the Arab Countries: A Case for Adaptation Governance and Leadership in Building Climate Resilience*. World Bank Publications, 2012.

"What Is Global Warming?" *National Geographic*, https://www.nationalgeographic.com/environment/global-warming/global-warming-overview/. Accessed 22 Nov. 2017.

World Health Organization (WHO). "Air Pollution Levels Rising In Many of The World's Poorest Cities," 12 May 2016. http://www.who.int/mediacentre/news/releases/2016/air-pollution-rising/en/

World Resources Institute. "Extreme Weather: What's Climate Change Got to Do With It?", 18 Sep. 2017. http://www.wri.org/blog/2017/09/extreme-weather-whats-climate-change-got-do-it.

PORTFOLIO FOUR

BY JORDYN HATCHER

WRT 150 gave Jordyn Hatcher, who studies mechanical engineering and math at Grand Valley, a chance to voice her opinion about issues that matter to her. Her first essay, "Doing It Like the Dutch," proposes that the United States adopt the Dutch system of sex education which focuses on early education on issues of both the biological and social elements of sexuality. Jordyn's second essay, "One Man's Perspective on Gender Equality," offers a carefully considered response to a TED Talk delivered by gender studies professor Michael Kimmel. Finally, Jordyn researches her own experience with sleep paralysis in "A Nightmare You Can't Wake Up From" to explore how this is a growing health concern, especially for college students.

While working on her essays in Professor Tamara Lubic's class, Jordyn chose to research topics that were personal to her, that she had a strong opinion on, and that she thought other students would relate to. The editors think you'll find her essays thought-provoking and engaging due to her interesting topic choices and her careful, thorough research.

Jordyn's Advice for WRT 150 Students

Do not procrastinate and go to the writing center.

DOING IT LIKE THE DUTCH

On more than several occasions, I have misinterpreted, misjudged, and misguided my peers on topics relevant to sex. It's almost as if we've been playing a game of telephone: facts change as it passes from one person to another. Why don't American teens, including myself, have a firm foundation of sex-related information? Who is to blame? Perhaps the U.S. policies on sex education within schools. In our country, only 24 states require sex education among adolescents; only 20 of them require HIV/AIDS accurate and factual education ("State Policies on Sex..."). Most programs within American schools only require abstinent-based education. Since the curriculum focuses on abstaining from sex, teens fail to learn about the precautions, safety, and resources available. Hormonal teenagers will, and do have sex; it is almost inevitable for some of them. Since they were not briefed on any aspects of sex in a professional and educational setting, they rely on their peers who may not have the most accurate advice. According to Sue Alford, writer for *Advocates for Youth*, the U.S. has the highest rate of teen pregnancies, teen births, teen abortions, HIV teen prevalence, and the lowest rate in the use of condoms and contraceptives compared to the Netherlands. Not only do the Dutch teach safe sex among teens, but they also teach personal and sexual growth/development. The U.S. should adopt these parameters; every state should be required to have sexuality education programs that includes abstinence as an option, but also focuses on contraception, safe sex, sexual development, gender identity, and healthy relationships. If I would have learned these aspects in high school, I feel that I would've benefited from them, especially now being in college, where sexual activity, varying sexual identities, and relationships are extremely prevalent.

Growing up in a town where sex education was not required has negatively affected me, along with thousands of other kids in the same predicament all around the country. I am from Maryland, and the only form of sex education I received was just learning about our anatomy; no one explained to me the confusing and hormonal feelings that were racing through my body. I was completely clueless trying to navigate puberty and the unexplained moods and

Contributed by Jordyn Hatcher. Copyright ©Kendall Hunt Publishing Company.

thoughts I had. I honestly didn't think I was normal or if anyone else was going through the same dilemma.

As I grew older I realized that, yes, everyone is in the same situation, but we've gained knowledge by word of mouth, not by a trained sex educator. We were never taught about safe sex, contraception, sexual identity, or HIV/AIDS. I was only taught to stay abstinent. When I moved to Michigan, I never took the high school's sex education class, but I looked up the requirements and according to Section 380.1507b in the *Michigan Legislature*, schools are only to teach the benefits of being abstinent, the dangers of teen sex and pregnancies, and how to say 'no' to sexual advances. It appears they are using a 'scare' tactic. This legislative document has not been updated in over 10 years, but times are changing and Michigan, along with the rest of the country, needs to update the sex education policies so teens can learn properly and openly about all aspects of sex.

Talk more / give more info on how the U.S. approaches sex ed. Introduce need for change

I interviewed a few of my peers, all from different high schools within Michigan, and concluded that they were all encouraged to not have sex. My friend, Kelly D'Angelo, a freshman at Grand Valley State University, said that "they mostly taught abstinence in [her] high school... and they never really talked about birth control or the Plan B pill." I asked my friend, Hannah Miller, what she wishes she would have learned in her health class. She responded, "I wish I knew what facilities are available for us girls... like where to get birth control... and how to have conversations about sex with our partners." Chris Maresh, a current senior at Lake Orion High School, wished he "would have learned different types of sexuality and gender identification. Being a gay male and not knowing the type of sexual options for me was really frightening." Out of all the other people I talked to, I can conclude that Michigan schools' sex education only focuses on abstinence, even though there is so much more to learn about sex. Although most teens practice abstinence, mainly because the scare tactics worked, they are still unaware of other aspects of sexuality. This can hinder them in the future. They wander obliviously through peak sexual ages without any guidance. They are embarrassed to ask questions; they don't feel comfortable talking about sex. The term and its discussion is taboo in America, but not so much in the Netherlands.

Get opinions/ thoughts from real students as evidence for the need for change in the U.S. sex ed. program

Contrary to the U.S., instead of teaching the dangers of sex, the Dutch teach the normal, positive aspects. The Netherlands is the most sexually-open country according to Alex Henderson, writer of the article, "5 Countries That Do It Better: How Sexual Prudery Makes America a Less Healthy and Happy Place." The Dutch comprehensive sexuality education starts as early as primary school. Of course, they do not teach kids about intercourse, but introduce healthy relationships, sexual preferences, and feelings leading up to sex. This implements an early, healthy, open-minded idea about sex and all its aspects to carry on through puberty. Saskia De Melker, writer for the *PBS News Hour*, states that:

> By law, all primary school students in the Netherlands must receive some form of sexuality education... they must address certain core principles — among them, sexual diversity and sexual assertiveness. [They] encourage respect for all sexual preferences and help kids develop skills to protect against sexual coercion, intimidation, and abuse. The underlying principle is straightforward: sexual development is a normal process that all young people experience, and they have the right to trustworthy information on the subject.

The requirements stated in the quote above is very beneficial for the students. It is extremely important, especially today, for kids to learn about sexual diversity. I recently watched an episode called, "The New Girl" of *The Mick*, a Fox television show, that addresses gender fluidity—which conveys a more flexible range of gender expression, with interests and behaviors that may change often, especially among kids ("Terminology"). In the episode, a 7-year-old Ben Pepperton, who is gender fluid, was expelled for inappropriate clothing and behavior. Principal Gibbons was not aware of this term but by the end of the episode, Ben was reinstated at his private school and his caregiver addressed gender fluidity to Gibbons and exclaimed, "You're an educator, educate yourself." This episode proves that our society is evolving, and we need an education system to match. Students as young as Ben Pepperton would benefit from this education, for they will continue developing these progressive mindsets as they grow older.

To move on from primary school sex education, the Netherlands do continue this program into secondary schooling. Just like any other subject, such as English or mathematics, these sexuality programs continue to build on top of the fundamentals taught in earlier years of schooling. Kelly J. Bell, a writer for the health sciences section of the *Inquires Journal*, states that there are six major themes taught in Dutch schools: Physical and Emotional

Development—this includes physical and emotional changes that happen among both sexes. Reproduction—accurate and simple language and diagrams to explain the act itself. *Weerbarheid* (interactional competence)—what students are comfortable with and how to be assertive in sexual situations. Relationships—covers heterosexual and homosexual relations. Sexuality—focuses on positive and pleasurable aspects, and Safe Sex—where to get contraception, how to use it, and what to do if nervous about asking for it. These six subjects are crucial for every adolescent to learn, especially at a rapidly developing age. American teens should reap the benefits of this form of education along with their Dutch peers. I and many others, would have greatly profited from a program that includes these ideas. This generation is one of the most progressive and it needs a sexual education course to keep up with its pace.

The Dutch sexuality education is extremely liberal and it may seem like a nightmare for many American parents. Some do not want their children exposed to the idea of sex and varying sexuality, let alone educating them at a much younger age. Most of the time it is due to religion—being homosexual is a sin and the idea of saving one's virginity till marriage is popular. Parents believe that if the ideas of sexuality are brought to the attention of their sons and daughters, then it will encourage them to act in such ways. But that is not always the case; if anything, teenagers tend to do the exact opposite of what they are told. Sexual preferences are predetermined and teens will have sex regardless of what is taught, so school programs might as well inform them about sexual diversity, the safety, and health precautions of sex.

The U.S. has the potential to better educate their kids about sexuality and make it less taboo, less promiscuous, and less confusing. Although the Netherland's form of sexuality education may seem like a complete 180-degree turn compared to America, it can be beneficial for the U.S. to gradually adapt to the Dutch program. Our country should slowly but surely make adjustments that contribute to today's kids and its surplus of diversity because we are becoming more advanced. We need to update laws and regulations that better suit our present society. I believe that proper, comprehensive, sexuality education can benefit the youth in several ways. It can lead to the obvious: fewer teen pregnancies, fewer teen births, and less HIV teen prevalence, but it can also lead to important intrinsic facets.

Word Count: 1620

Works Cited

Alford, Sue. "Adolescent Sexual Health in Europe and the US." *Advocates for Youth*, March 2011. http://www.advocatesforyouth.org/publications/419-adolescent-sexual-health-in-europe-and-the-us. Accessed 6 Feb. 2017.

Bell, Kelly J. "Wake Up and Smell the Condoms: An Analysis of Sex Education Programs in the United States, the Netherlands, Sweden, Australia, France, and Germany." *Inquires.* vol 1, no. 11, https://www.inquiriesjournal.com/articles/40/wake-up-and-smell-the-condoms-an-analysis-of-sex-education-programs-in-the-united-states-the-netherlands-sweden-australia-france-and-germany. Accessed 27 Mar. 2017

Bell, Taylor. "How Europe Proves That U.S. Sex Education Sucks." *Sex Education in Europe vs. the U.S.,* 4 Apr. 2016. http://www.attn.com/stories/7020/sex-education-europe-compared-to-united-states.

D'Angelo, Kelly. Personal Interview. 13 Feb. 2017.

De Melker, Saskia. "The Case for Starting Sex Education in Kindergarten." *PBS News Hour.* Public Media WGVU, 27 May 2015. http://www.pbs.org/newshour/updates/spring-fever/.

Henderson, Alex. "5 Countries That Do It Better: How Sexual Prudery Makes America a Less Healthy and Happy Place." *ALTERNET.* 12 Apr. 2012. http://www.alternet.org/story/154970/5_countries_that_do_it_better%3A_how_sexual_prudery_makes_america_a_less_healthy_and_happy_place.

Maresh, Chris. Personal Interview. 12 Apr. 2017.

Miller, Hannah. Personal Interview. 14 Feb. 2017.

NowThis. "Which Countries Have the Best Sex Education?" *YouTube,* commentary by Evan Puschak, 13 May 2015. https://www.youtube.com/watch?v=UBDBLQ8vXC8.

"Section 380.1507b." *Michigan Legislature*, 24 June 2004, www.legislature.mi.gov/(S(rgkwjwh43kf2pjcl5fhi2loi))/mileg.aspx?page=GetObject&objectname=mcl-380-1507b. Accessed 12 Mar. 2017.

"State Policies on Sex Education in Schools." *National Conference of State Legislators,* NCSL, 16 Feb. 2016. http://www.ncsl.org/research/health/state-policies-on-sex-education-in-schools.aspx.

"Terminology." *Gender Diversity*, 2017. http://www.genderdiversity.org/resources/terminology/#genderfluidity. Accessed 12 Mar. 2017.

"The New Girl." *The Mick,* written by Dave and John Chernin, season 1, episode 11, FOX, 2017.

ONE MAN'S PERSPECTIVE ON GENDER EQUALITY

Living in an era of one of the biggest civil rights movement, it is almost impossible to go a day without hearing issues pertaining to gender equality. This topic, which I have only heard women discuss, has an unlikely representative: Michael Kimmel, a white middle-class male. He is a researcher, a writer—books about men and masculinity—and a professor, specializing in gender studies at Stony Brook University (Kimmel). He presented his TED Talk entitled, "Why Gender Equality Is Good for Everyone: Men Included," at TEDWomen in 2015, a conference held to discuss gender issues. In his talk Kimmel addresses, with humor and personal anecdotes, invisible privilege and how gender equality can be beneficial for men. Overall, I thought the presentation was appealing and comical, but as I mulled over the points Kimmel provided, I realized that his approach to engage men in promoting gender equality is contradictory. Gender equality is to help women preserve their rights as humans, yet Kimmel makes his talk exclusively about men and the benefits they will receive.

To begin his talk, Kimmel starts off by delivering a narrative of how he came to realize his privilege. Back when he first started teaching, he belonged to a group of women who discussed different ideologies and hosted potlucks. He attended a get-together and listened to a conversation between two women. A black woman asked a white woman what she saw in the mirror. They white woman responded by saying just a woman. The black woman then stated, "'You see, that's the problem for me. Because when… I look in the mirror… I see a *black* woman. To me, race is visible. But to you, race is invisible. You don't see it.'" Kimmel then addresses the audience and declares, "…that's how privilege works. Privilege is invisible to those who have it. It is a luxury…" I have never thought of putting it that way, but privilege is precisely that: imperceptible to those who have it.

Growing up a minority—a woman of color—I always assumed everyone thought like me. I was extremely conscious of race and frequently kept tabs on others around me and the pigment of their skin. In school, I noticed that I didn't look like most of the kids surrounding me since I grew up in white suburbia; I stuck out like a sore thumb. When I look in the mirror I see a *brown* girl. I can't imagine identifying myself any other way, I couldn't imagine identifying myself as just a girl. Recently, I've been addressing my white friends about race—conclusively, none of them really have to be cognizant of the color of their skin. That right there to me, is privilege. I'm jealous that most of my white peers never need to worry about walking into a place and being self-conscious about every move they make in fear of getting judged merely based on their skin tone. They rarely think about being susceptible to certain things—shoplifting or other malicious behavior—because of the color of their skin. They seldom worry about being rejected because of their ethnicity since white is the standard. Miki Kashtan, a writer for the *Fearless Heart*, offers her own take on the subject by saying, "As a person with fairly light skin… I have access to untold number of privileges that are mine to enjoy and which are not available to people with darker skin. I can, as a very simple example, go in and out of stores without having security officers look at my movements." All white women have this luxury, but white men have it even better. Kimmel addresses this by continuing his story. He speaks to the audience and says that he had an epiphany when the white woman answered the black woman. When he looks in the mirror, he just sees a human being—one with no gender or race. He is "universally generalizable" (Kimmel). White men don't have to worry about being discriminated against for being a certain gender or certain race. They have the most privilege of any human and, for the most part, none of them recognize this.

Kimmel moves away from his first point, privilege, and goes into his second—double standards in society among men and women. According to Breana Brills, a instructor for Niles West High school, this term means "an action or event that becomes a norm for one gender, but not the other." Kimmel then provides a time where he's experienced a double standard. Two professors, him and a woman, same class: gender studies. To the students, the female professor appeared to be biased and opinionated when talking about structural inequality in the United States, whereas when Kimmel lectured the class about the same topic, the students took his statements as facts. Simply because the first professor was the female, students automatically created a standard that made her seem unqualified. I agree that there are some double standards among men and women, but nowadays, it's not as much of a predominant problem, especially as time progresses. My engineering lecturer, Professor

Katherine Christopher (KC), is a young woman, and on the first day of class, when she walked to the front, murmurs spread across the room and my peers were saying, 'she must be another TA' or 'what is she doing up there?' No one expected a young female professor for an engineering class. Professor KC, nonetheless, taught the class, impressed all the females, along with her colleagues, who were in the room observing. Most of the men in my class did not think any less of her, but there were a few opponents who were still critical. Unfortunately, some men are stubborn to change their patriarchal views. Kimmel addresses these type of men as the opposition group.

Kimmel starts talking about a specific group of men that resist gender equality. This group applied to jobs that were taken by their female counterparts. They had a talk show called, 'A Black Woman Took *My* Job' to address their discomfort in not getting their desired position. The title, itself, is alarming. First, is there a need to identify such a race and gender? And secondly, which Kimmel also addresses, what is with the word, '*my*'? In the title, the connotation behind this word suggests that the job belonged to them to begin with. Where did this sense of entitlement come from? Why did these men assume the job was already theirs? Kimmel states that men grow up being the norm and expect all aspects of society to be in their favor. Without confronting their sense of entitlement, we will never understand why so many men resist gender equality. It seems to them as if they are getting robbed. Men have thought for years that they are on a level playing field, so when any policy tilts against them, even a little bit, they think it's reverse discrimination (Kimmel). This makes sense to me. If I were used to certain ways and the minute something changes, making me give up some of things that I've been entitled to, I would think it is reverse discrimination as well. It's very subjective and relative to what people are accustomed to, but it important to call out men on their entitlements, just like Kimmel says. Otherwise, they will go their entire lives being ignorant to the existence of their prerogatives. Kimmel then relates his two points, privilege and double standards, and makes the claim that making gender visible to men is the first step to engaging men to support gender equality. Men must acknowledge their invisible privilege to understand and fully encourage equality among women (Kimmel). It is a struggle to do so and it can be difficult to involve men in an issue they don't even realize is happening.

Kimmel finishes addressing the obstacles of engaging men and starts to go into the benefits men can get out of gender equality. He states that it "is actually a way for [men] to get the lives [they] want..." The examples Kimmel gives are things like, a better sex life or a healthier marriage. Although I agree with this statement, it bothers me because he is suggesting that men are still the center of concern. Meaning, for men to get what *they* want, *they* should want gender equality, not because they deem it as fair for women. They look at it in their own self-interest. And of course, a white male, though very thoughtful and deeply engaged in the movement, Kimmel still makes remarks that are not exactly going about gender equality. He also talks about how equality can be great for business. Again, he is trying to find other ways to let men know that equality can be beneficial for them. His approach to engage men is skewed to look like it will benefit men instead of telling them that they should just believe in it because it's the most humane and equitable thing to do. There are much bigger issues to address like violence against women or equal education for girls, rather than just a happy wife or a better sex life, like Kimmel suggests are the benefits for men. According to Elli Scambor and Nadja Bergmann, contributing authors of the *Men and Masculinities* journal, the "most serious causes of gender inequality [are] violent acts (physical, psychological, and sexual) [which are] performed everywhere (in public places, workplaces, and in intimate relationships) [and] are committed by men tied to traditional gender roles." Violence is what the focus should be on. This is what should be used to persuade men to promote equality. My personal priority is not about the benefits men can get from gender equality, but decreasing the inequality upon women. I feel that the women's benefits significantly outweigh the men's benefits, especially since women have been deemed inferior for hundreds of years. I understand that Kimmel is trying to connect and persuade men to support gender equality but it troubles me that men must be persuaded into a movement that they should fully support regardless. Overall, I agree with Kimmel's statement on how privilege is invisible and how gender equality can be great for men, but the way he approaches it makes the topic seem more about men than women. Like the Black Lives Matter movement, people are not saying that black lives matter more than everybody else's, they are just saying that black lives are in more jeopardy compared to everybody else and we should focus on their wellbeing. Women's inequality is so prevalent today and our nation needs to focus on that.

Word Count: 1767

Works Cited

Brill, Breana. "Gender Inequality: The Double Standard." *Niles West News.* 15 Jan. 2014. http://www.nileswestnews.org/west-word/gender-inequality-the-double-standard.

Kashtan, Miki. "Invisible Power and Privilege." *The Fearless Heart.* 28 June 2011. http://thefearlessheart.org/invisible-power-and-privilege.

Kimmel, Michael. "Why Gender Equality is Good for Everyone—Men Included." *TED*, May 2015. https://www.ted.com/speakers/michael_kimmel.

Scambor, Elli and Nadja Bergmann, et. al. "Men and Gender Equality: European Insights." *Men and Masculinities,* vol. 17, num. 5, 2014, pp 562-563. *SAGE.* http://journals.sagepub.com/doi/pdf/10.1177/1097184X14558239. Accessed 29 Jan. 2017.

A NIGHTMARE I CAN'T WAKE UP FROM

I am asleep, dreaming of being on a deserted beach flourishing with palm trees and tropical foliage, lounging in a reclined chair, and the sun kissing my skin. The waves roll and the seagulls chirp. It is peaceful. Then suddenly, I am immersed in darkness; gray clouds appear in the sky, the waves grow bigger—sloshing onto shore, and gusts of wind blow by. Thunder booms and lightning strikes. The urge to wake up is resonant, but I remain on the beach—trapped. For some reason, the sensations of my real-life surroundings are identified while simultaneously staying on the beach. My cotton sheets lay beneath me and the white noise of my fan buzzes. I know I am awake; at least my mind is. I try to open my eyes but they are sealed shut. I try to move my arms but they remain dormant. My heart is racing as I attempt to wake myself up. It feels as though the world is weighing on my chest. My breath shortens. I'm no longer on the beach, I'm now in complete darkness. It is an out-of-body experience: I see myself lying in my twin bed nestled in the corner of my room. My mind is active—conscious— while my body is still sleeping. It seems as if I am trapped forever in this in-between-world of slumber and consciousness. I can't do anything about it, except wait. Wait for someone to wake me or wait for this nightmare to be over. This incident is known as the phenomenon, sleep paralysis. Some may argue that sleep paralysis isn't a serious condition, but I beg to differ. Not only is sleep paralysis a sleep disorder, it is also linked to depression—being one of the side effects.

Sleep paralysis is a recurrent inability to move the body at sleep onset or upon awakening, according to Monica Liskova and Denisa Janeckova, authors of, "The Episode and Predictive Factors of Sleep Paralysis in University Students." There are two types: hypnagogic (falling asleep) and hypnopompic (awaking from sleep), the most common type encountered being the latter ("Sleep Paralysis"). Episodes can last up to a few minutes, though it may seem much longer. During an episode, people are unable to move their body, speak, and in some cases, unable to open their eyes (Liskova and Janeckova). Victims often express that there is a weighted impression on their chest or experience a choking sensation around their neck. Hallucinations of devilish beings are extremely common as well. These effects are often why sleep paralysis is compared to a feeling close to death. I would describe it as death's cousin.

Sleep paralysis has been known about and recorded for hundreds of years all around the world due to its death-like quality. The earliest accounts can be found in a Chinese book of dream documentations dating back to 400 B.C. (MacKinnon). One of the most historic visual examples is a portrait entitled, "The Nightmare," painted by Swiss artist, Henry Fuseli, in 1781 (Figure 1). The photo below represents the ambiance of an episode. A dragon lurks behind blood-red drapes and a grotesque gremlin-like creature sits on top of a woman laying on a bed in a dimly-lit room. This represents the devilish presence and a heavy chest sensation that one feels during an episode. Hallucinations such as these are extremely common. According to Alina Bradford, writer for *Live Science*, people encounter hallucinations since the mind is still in dream-state. People have reported seeing ghosts, demons, and other strange

Figure 1 The Nightmare, 1781 (oil on canvas), Fuseli, Henry (Fussli, Johann Heinrich) (1741–1825) / Detroit Institute of Arts, USA / Founders Society Purchase with funds from Mr. and Mrs. Bert L. Smokler and Mr. and Mrs. Lawrence A. Fleischmanf / Bridgeman Images

apparitions (Bradford). Sleep paralysis was known as the "original nightmare." The suffix -*mare* derives from the Norse word *mara*: a supernatural being, usually female, that lays on people's chests at night creating shortness in breath and suffocation (MacKinnon). The term "nightmare" has since been altered to what people know it by today. That is why so many people are not familiar with the term, sleep paralysis.

Although, sleep paralysis has existed for centuries, it hasn't been a familiar phenomenon therefore, there aren't any studies tested on large groups. A'ndrea Messer, author of the Penn State article entitled, "Sleep Paralysis More Common in Students," found that there are studies on individual groups of people based on different ethnicities, ages, and psychiatric debilities. It has been calculated that only 8% of the population face sleep paralysis; students and mental patients making up most of that percentage (Messer). 28% of university students and 35% of psychiatric patients have reported experiencing episodes; these statistics are relatively high compared to other individual groups that were tested. University students and psychiatric patients are the predominant groups, both having high rates of depression now more than ever, according to Joel Brown, writer of "Anxiety: The Most Common Mental Health Diagnosis in College Students." There appears to be a correlation between sleep paralysis and depression.

Most college-aged students are aware of the "original nightmare," compared to older generations. This is because university students have gone through episodes more often than any other group, besides psychiatric patients. Students are also one of the highest groups that have depression. The 2015 chart of depressive episodes (Figure 2) on the next page, developed by the National Institute of Mental Health, shows that adults, 18-25, have the highest rate. I suffered from depression in my senior year of high school and that is when sleep paralysis was extremely prevalent in my life. It became so habitual that I refused to sleep some nights. Eventually, I took the liberty of looking up tips on how to cope.

Sleep paralysis is usually a one-time event; but in special cases, it can happen quite often for some people. The only thing sufferers can do is wait it out and learn how to cope like I did. Ryan Hurd, writer of the *Dream Studies Portal* article, "9 Ways to Wake Up from Sleep Paralysis" offers victims a few tips. The most common are: clenching fists and wiggling fingers and toes. Others that he listed include: don't fight it, give in, focus on breathing, coughing, and

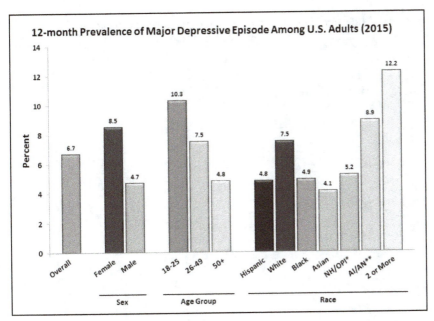

Figure 2 Major Depressive Episodes Among Adults ("Major")

scrunching up the face. I have done these and they have all worked for me, especially not focusing on breathing. Keeping the mind preoccupied on something other than panicking is the best way to break from an episode. I have mastered the art of waking up, mostly because I've had practice.

Much like me, Brandon Spoolstra, a fellow student at Grand Valley State University, has experienced numerous episodes of sleep paralysis. The first few times he remembers experiencing the phenomenon was when he was 17 and 20 years old. Spoolstra has suffered from depression in the past, and has recently been a victim of stress, especially since starting a new job. He says that "it's been very demanding." The most recent incident he had was Sunday, March 19, 2017. He hadn't been sleeping very well and decided to go to his friend's apartment. Fortunately, he could fall asleep almost effortlessly on his friend's couch. Sadly, upon awakening he felt as though he were stuck to the sofa. He couldn't open his eyes nor speak. He did, however, hear and sense everything around him. His friend came over and adjusted his blanket, unaware that Spoolstra was experiencing such a terror. But just by the mere touch of his friend, Spoolstra could wake the rest of his body up. He recalls,

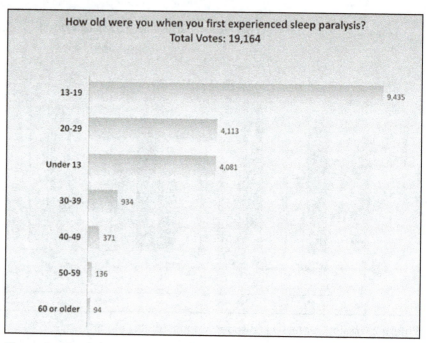

Figure 3   Age First Experienced (Green)

"It's pure panic. It feels like someone pinned you down and you just want to be able to move."

In a recent lecture Spoolstra and I attended, my professor was shocked by how many students were familiar and/or associated with sleep paralysis. Several of my peers offered up their experiences. It was very intriguing to hear some of their stories, so much so I wanted to hear more. I visited many websites and read personal accounts of others who've battled with incidences. I saw that most were college-aged adults. A poll (Figure 3) conducted by Ethan Green, founder of the website, "No Sleepless Nights," displays that people 29 and younger have had an episode more so than people older than 30—the highest rate being found in the age interval 13-19.

Teens along with university students have the highest prevalence rate of sleep paralysis compared to any other age group. A study conducted by Mariana Szklo-Coxe, Terry Young, Laurel Finn, and Emmanuel Mignot for the National Institutes of Health, explores depression and its link to sleep disturbances. They found that sleep paralysis is strongly associated with depression even when they took out variables such as antidepressants, daytime sleepiness, and insomnia (Szklo-Coxe, et al.). Although this study is from 2007, the conclusion remains relevant since depression doesn't alter: the effects are identical even 10 years later. Luckily, not all victims of depression go through such a horrific terror, but the few that due have never been more terrified in their life.

Sleep paralysis has been known and expressed as a night terror that can't compare to anything else. The inability to move, the shortness of breath, and the demonizing aura that accompanies sleep paralysis has terrified many. Through the centuries, people of all different cultures have experienced this phenomenon and have documented them differently, but we can all agree, it's an unfathomable nightmare. Sleep paralysis is a very real and frightening thing I've experienced, along with several others who have also suffered from depression. As it becomes a more predominant issue in society, I'm hopeful that there will be more conclusive studies and information provided for victims.

Word Count: 1580

Works Cited

Bradford, Alina. "Sleep Paralysis: Causes, Symptoms and Treatments." *Live Science*, Purch, 19 May 2015, www.livescience.com/50876-sleep-paralysis.html.

Brown, Joel. "Anxiety: The Most Common Mental Health Diagnosis in College Students." *BU Today*, Boston University, 10 Feb. 2016, www.bu.edu/today/2016/college-students-anxiety-and-depression/.

Fuseli, Henry. "The Nightmare." *Detroit Institute of Arts*. http://www.dia.org/object-info/f222b80e-c3ba-4dd0-a705-4b14cb4f5ad6.aspx. Accessed 22 Mar. 2017.

Green, Ethan. "Sleep Paralysis Stories - The Scariest Sleep Disorder of All." *No Sleepless Nights*, 13 Dec. 2016, www.nosleeplessnights.com/sleep-paralysis-stories-intruder-demon-or-delusion/.

Hillin, Taryn. "Why People with Sleep Paralysis See the Supernatural." *Fusion*, 6 Sept. 2015, http://fusion.net/story/145337/why-people-with-sleep-paralysis-see-supernatural-visions/.

Hurd, Ryan. "9 Ways to Wake Up from Sleep Paralysis." *Dream Studies Portal*, 2014, http://dreamstudies.org/2010/04/29/9-ways-to-wake-up-from-sleep-paralysis/. Accessed 3 Apr. 2017.

Liskova, Monica and Denisa Janeckova, et al. "The Episode and Predictive Factors of Sleep Paralysis in University Students." *PMC*, Neuropsychiatric Disease & Treatment, vol. 12, Nov. 2016, https://www.ncbi.nlm.nih.gov/pmc/articles/PMC5115681/.

MacKinnon, Carla. "Culture and History." *The Sleep Paralysis Project*, Royal College of Art, June 2015, www.thesleepparalysisproject.org/about-sleep-paralysis/culture-and-history/.

"Major Depression Among Adults." *National Institutes of Health*, U.S. Department of Health and Human Services, 2015, www.nimh.nih.gov/health/statistics/prevalence/major-depression-among-adults.shtml. Accessed 12 Mar. 2017.

Messer, A'ndrea Elyse. "Sleep Paralysis More Common in Students." *Futurity*, Pennsylvania State University, 21 Oct. 2011, http://www.futurity.org/sleep-paralysis-more-common-in-students/. Accessed 12 Mar. 2017

"Sleep Paralysis." *WebMD*, www.webmd.com/sleep-disorders/guide/sleep-paralysis. Accessed 3 Apr. 2017.

Spoolstra, Brandon. Personal Interview. 22 Mar. 2017.

Szklo-Coxe, Mariana, and Terry Young, et al. "Depression: Relationships to Sleep Paralysis and Other Sleep Disturbances in a Community Sample." *Journal of Sleep Research*, U.S. National Library of Medicine, 2007, www.ncbi.nlm.nih.gov/pmc/articles/PMC2800990/. Accessed 12 Mar. 2017.

PORTFOLIO FIVE

BY KYLE CHRISTIE

Kyle Christie, a psychology and behavioral neuroscience double major, used his own experiences as a starting point for the essays he wrote in Sister Lucia Treanor's WRT 150 class. His first essay, "Two in the Same," is a personal narrative that vividly describes his experiences as a student with autism. As Kyle reflected, this was "the first time I ever wrote about my Asperger's, but it . . . helped shed some light on this condition for students who don't know it by name." Kyle's second essay, "Formation and Foundation," evaluates a piece of art many of GVSU students might be familiar with, the mural "Foundation" that hangs in the Loutit Lecture Hall in Henry Hall on campus. Finally, Kyle's portfolio ends with his persuasive essay, "The Sound of Silence," which argues for more funding for the arts in high schools.

Like many students in WRT 150, Kyle found that peer review workshops were his favorite part of the class. He recalls, "It became very interesting to see how different people related to your essay . . . and it made you take other's opinions into consideration to make your essays more well rounded." It was clear to the editors that Kyle was keenly aware of other readers when he wrote and revised his essays—he chose interesting topics, researched them carefully, and wrote about them clearly and persuasively.

Kyle's Advice for WRT 150 Students

Write what you want to write about in the way you want to write about it. Anyone can find sources and summarize them, and then cite them accordingly. Passion, dedication, and voice is not something that can be taught, and is often times what turns a good essay into a great one. If you enjoy what you're writing about, others will enjoy reading it. As for the things that helped me be successful, plan your time wisely and have your paper exposed to as many people and critiques as possible. The former will ensure that what you're writing is at your highest quality, while the latter will expose you to new ideas that you many not have been exposed to before.

TWO IN THE SAME

"Ass burgers?" my confused 6-year-old self said, "does that mean I have hamburgers on my butt?". I quickly checked my back side to see if the previous statement was true. It was not. My mother chuckled at my childish ignorance, but her smile quickly faded into an apathetic face. "You have something called Asperger's syndrome," she said, putting extra emphasis on the 'p' this time. "It's a form of autism." While this might seem like a scary thing to hear, I did not quite understand the denotation of the word *autism*, so I simply brushed it off. I soon wished I could brush off my Asperger's like I did when I was six.

I began to think of my autism as my conjoined twin. After all, it's not like he could be removed from me. As far as most people were concerned, we were the same age, height, even had the same type of dirty blonde hair and brown-green hazel eyes. However, in terms of personality, we were as dissimilar as identical twins could possibly be. When I wanted to learn from my mistakes, he would throw a tantrum. When I wanted to speak clearly, he would want to jumble up my words. When I wanted to tackle new tasks and places with enthusiasm, he would fill me with anxiety and fear. When I wanted to be sociable with other people, he would force me to hide and be secluded. Throughout my life, we waged a civil war in which the winner would get to be Kyle's personality. Most of the time, my autism would win the battle.

The first battle my autism won was during a preschool science demonstration. It was simple, each kid was given an item and had to determine whether it would float or sink. Then the kids would proceed to drop the item into a bucket of water to see whether their guess was right. My item was grapes, and since I associated an object's buoyancy with success, I was positive that my grapes would float. After watching the first grape sink, I was stunned; it must have been a bad grape. I dropped another grape, and once again, it sank to the bottom. *These grapes have to float, there's no way I could be wrong*, I thought to myself. I picked up another grape, broke it in half, and then slowly and carefully placed each half in the water. I watched as each half methodically sank to the bottom of the bucket once again. My autism went crazy. I started crying and screaming at the top of my lungs. The instructor tried to help calm me down, but it only made it worse. I ran to the bathroom and locked the door so I could cry by myself for the next 30 minutes.

My autism was a perfectionist; anytime I did something wrong, or got out in a game in gym, the response would always be to cry. However, I soon figured out that crying because you were wrong is frowned upon and is usually followed by being labeled a "crybaby." Luckily, I was able to find a loophole which allowed me cry when I would get "out" playing a game in gym. I realized that crying because you were injured was more acceptable than crying because you got out, so I would fake an injury and cry because I was "injured." I did it so often and got so good at it that both my instructors and parents were worried about my well-being. They were so concerned that my parents bought me a kid-sized Michigan football helmet to wear during recess and gym to help protect my head from any serious damage. Now not only was I a crybaby, but also the weird guy who wore a football helmet during recess. Just when I thought I had the upper hand, my autism won another battle.

As you can imagine, my autism made it extremely hard to make friends (a helmet wearing crybaby usually does not scream "friend material"). This made transitioning from grade to grade extremely hard. Each one presented me with new instructors and people, creating a new environment filled with anxiety. I tried to do anything and everything to make people like me and want to be my friend. I would eat paper so that people would know me and refer to me as "the paper eater" rather than "crybaby". I would tell lies and make up stories that I lived a life I could only dream of and had the coolest parents ever just to make people interested in what I had to say.

While it provided me with instant gratification, in the end I still did not have any close friends. I would spend some nights crying because of that. I kept asking the person beyond the clouds, whoever it was, why I was so weird and why I could not meet anyone else like me. Then I realized that the only person that was like me was me, my autism. I figured out that I could not spend all this time fighting with myself because we were not two people, but one. We were two in the same. Instead of clashing personalities, I tried combining them. I took the perfectionist side of my autism and mixed it with my ability to understand that I will make mistakes and can learn from them. I took my over emotional side from my autism and used it to satisfy my urge to connect with other people. For the first time, I finally started to accept my autism as part of me.

However, learning to live with my autism instead of fighting against it was no easy task. I had to seek help from trained professionals in order to shift this perspective. In first grade, I started going to counseling every Wednesday after school. While I can't recall the actual "counseling process", what I do remember is playing a variety of board games. This might seem strange at first, but I soon came to realize that these games made me feel comfortable and relaxed in this new environment that otherwise would have given me anxiety. During these sessions, I would talk about how my day went, what I was going to be doing that weekend, or asked any questions that my young mind thought of. With help from the counselor, I started finding new ways to deal with exciting situations. Rather than walking on my tip toes or flapping my hands, I learned to contain my excitement and do mannerisms that were more common. These counseling sessions made new environments seem less threating to me and made me feel that I could apply myself in more diverse situations.

Another challenge I had to overcome was a slight speech impediment. As I grew up, I had a difficult time enunciating the letter "r". This led to words like rabbit to sound more like "wabbit". As a result, I would get mocked a lot in elementary school as my words sounded funny. This made me a lot less eager to socialize with others. In order to combat this, I was assigned a speech pathologist around second grade. The speech pathologist gave me a packet with various words and pictures that contained the letter r. She then showed me where to position my tongue to form the "r" sound, followed by her saying the word correctly. After she was done, I was given a mirror to see if my tongue was in the right place, and then I would proceed to say the word. At first it was frustrating. I was doing everything right, but it just didn't sound the same. At home, my mom and I would practice this same method every day for about 30 minutes. Surely but slowly, I started naturally moving my tongue in the right position and no longer needed the mirror. I could say each word in the packet correctly without any hesitation. I became more confident in my speaking ability, and my need to socialize became greater.

With help from these professionals, I started to learn how to cope with my autism. I became more sociable and started to find common interests with my other classmates, such as playing the same video games or finding out that other people liked to drink the carbonated "fizz" after you pour a soda. I was not crying or faking injuries anymore and I excelled in school. I started to apply myself to new situations I never thought I could. These transitions became easier and now I loved going to new places and meeting new people. I started to feel like I was finally fitting in for the first time.

If we were friends, or even if we had a casual conversation today, chances are you would never know that I have autism. My eyes might drift from maintaining eye contact with you, or I might ramble and stutter a little bit, but nothing too extreme. You might even notice that I have huge calf muscles from walking on my tiptoes, but you would never know why. Other than that, I have been extremely successful coping with it. Having autism gives me a unique perspective. I can understand the feelings that both autistic and non-autistic kids experience and can personally relate to them. This has helped me to connect with even more people and be more understanding of other's emotions. My autism went from a hindrance that would not go away, to a unique gift that I would not trade for the world.

Contrary to what we are taught in our history classes, not all wars have victors and losers. Sometimes the opposing sides realize that the war is not worth fighting and decide to reach an agreement. Such was the case between me and my autism. We did not need to fight a "civil war," we just had to understand each other better. In hindsight, I am still glad I had all these problems when I was younger. The struggles I went through made me the person I am today, and for that, I am thankful. Remembering these stories always brings a smile to my face as they were little battles that I thought I had to conquer. I realize that I tried too hard to fit in when I was made to stand out. Perhaps my 6-year-old self was on to something when I first heard that I had Asperger's. I did not panic; I did not cry; I did not get angry. I simply just brushed it off and went on with the rest of my day. Even today, I do the exact same thing. I just imagine my autism as nothing serious and I never let it bring me down. Opposite to what I thought when I was younger, my autism is not a conjoined twin or even an archenemy in a war. My autism is simply a unique part of me; it is a part of who I am.

Word Count: 1842

FORMATION AND FOUNDATION

As is the case on many campuses, artwork is evident in many aspects of the college experience. Grand Valley is no exception. Very rarely, however, is a work of art a piece of a building, let alone an entire wall. In the Loutit Lecture Hall of Henry Hall there is a 40-foot-long mural that is composed of almost 1,000 individually crafted six-inch by six-inch clay tiles. Each tile is either carved or casted with objects relating to science including various scientific tools, equations, atomic names of elements, and even names of famous scientists (See Appendix A, Figure 1). Simply and appropriately called *Formation*, this piece is the result of a three-year long project headed by artist Daleene Menning. *Formation* captures the attention of nearly everyone who walks by it, whether it be from its sheer size, the multi-colored clay tiles, or even the three-dimensional, tactile effect that the piece gives off. It is almost impossible to turn a blind eye to this artwork.

While there is a lot to be visually discovered, including its unique shape from the curved wall, I wondered about the process of creating this work. I pondered why clay was chosen as the medium for this piece, or why all the tiles were science related. In order to satisfy my curiosity, I interviewed Menning, both via email and face-to-face, in order to understand as much as I possibly could. After both interviews and summaries of the piece, I was able to obtain enough information to evaluate critically three things that stood out to me: the genre of this piece, its name, and the medium chosen.

Most works of art are usually classified by genre, or similar themes and concepts shared between them. However, with a piece as unique as *Formation*, finding similarities with other pieces was difficult. This may be attributed to Menning's understanding of art. When asked to define the genre, she stated that she doesn't think of art in that way, and that *Formation* is "a very individual response to a commission with a purpose" (Menning, email). Since *Formation* is not defined by a specific genre, it allows the observers to interpret the art in their own way, and assign a genre that matches their unique viewpoint. Nonetheless, viewers can still define *Formation* in a general sense as both academic and modern. It is academic because it represents the various sciences that are taught today. This work is a prominent display of academia, giving the observer many small snapshots of the great big world of science. Menning was tasked with creating a mural for science in general, which is how *Formation* came to be. As a result, she had to interpret what "science" really meant to her. This is important since modern art is defined as an "artist's intent to portray a subject as it exists in the world, according to his or her unique perspective" ("modern art" 1). This means that science was the subject, and *Formation* was how Menning interpreted it. Also, since the piece was completed in 1996, this recent work of art is considered modern. With *Formation* being such a unique piece, it is hard to pinpoint one single genre for it. Perhaps it is a "formation" of multiple genres, and it is up to the observer to decide.

All puns aside, the name *Formation* holds significant importance for this piece. This might seem abnormal since most clay works, such as pottery, are meant to be either visually pleasing or used as tools. In a general sense, many assume that the name "formation" simply comes from the formation of the hundreds of tiles to create the giant mural. However, the greatest works of art tend to run deeper than their superficial meaning. Menning stated that "the name 'formation' was given to the work as it is about the formation of the earth and the universe" (Menning, email). More specifically, *Formation* deals with the widely-known theory of the organization of the universe called the "Big Bang Theory". The theory states that all the materials that were necessary for the creation of the universe were already in a single spot. When the heat and pressure of the materials became too great for the single spot, there was a huge outward explosion, which then created our every expanding universe. Menning took this idea and incorporated it as an homage to Grand Valley's numerous scientific disciplines. Like the random particles that came together to form the universe, the artist symbolically recreated the event by fashioning the tiles containing multiple aspects of science non-specifically. As a result, Menning was able to create her own "big bang."

Arguably, the most important aspect of the mural is its medium, which is clay. During the construction of Padnos Hall of Science, there was a deposit of over four tons of glacier clay in the dig site. It was at first seen as a nuisance for construction. However, a former science dean wondered whether the clay could be given to an artist who could create a work of art to commemorate the completion of the building (Menning, personal). Once Menning was selected for the job, the process of making the clay suitable for casting began. One of the problems with the glacier clay was that the fine particles made it plastic, but also very fragile. Thus, the glacier clay had to be mixed with other industrial clay materials so it would not break. The clay tiles in *Formation* can be broken down into two categories, impression and casting. Casting is a complex process that involves building a clay wall around the object and then filling the walled area with plaster. Once the plaster dries, the surrounding wall gets broken down, and hopefully there is a good casting of the object. Impressing is a simpler process of taking an object and imprinting it onto wet clay. This is helpful for objects, like the computer keyboard (See Appendix A, Figure 2), in which the plaster would get between the cracks of the keys (Menning, email). This process was repeated over 1500 times to guarantee enough tiles for the projects. Once they were all casted or imprinted, it was time for the clay to get fired

The firing process brought a whole new set of hurdles to get over. One of the biggest problems with clay is that it shrinks in the kiln. In fact, estimates placed the shrink rate of clay at about 17%. Menning, however, did not have to worry about that when it came to *Formation's* tiles. "You have to worry about clay shrinkage when you're making things like a pitcher with a lid," she stated, "but with things like these, you can't really tell if it shrunk" (Menning, personal). Even after the tiles went through the kiln and shrunk, they presented more troubles; the tiles were coming out in multiple colors. Menning recalled that the first couple of tiles were dark black, but as she went on, they started being multiple colors. These included whites, blacks, and light brown and light reds (See Appendix A, Figure 3). The multiple colors of the tiles resulted from tiny veins of red and black iron ores that were not visible until after the firing process. While this might worry many artists, it did not faze Menning at all. "You have to have a certain degree of confidence in your creative ability and in your problem-solving ability," she explained, "I had confidence that I could make it do what I wanted it to do in the end. I'm glad now in hindsight that it multicolored because it helped fit the concept of science and its generalities in all that can happen and go wrong" (Menning, personal). Perhaps that is why both science and *Formation* is so interesting. Neither went exactly as planned, but each resulted in a beautiful creation that is meant to be admired.

Formation is a masterfully crafted mural that contains many secrets and hidden meanings if one is willing to look for them. The multi-assorted colors and three-dimensional tiles help capture the attention of anyone who walks by. Perhaps the most fascinating thing about *Formation* is its inclusions of aspects from all types of sciences. The wall almost serves as a benchmark for scientific literacy, as the more classes students take, the more tiles they can understand. *Formation* has been a part of Grand Valley's Henry Hall from the beginning, and accurately suggests the formation of the sciences that the university has to offer. Its rich symbolism, history, and scientific information is unmatched by any other work at the university.

Word Count: 1433

Works Cited

Menning, Daleene. "Daleene Menning - Formation Mural." *Daleene Menning - Mural*, daleenemenning.com/Formation. htm. Website of Artist.

-----. Email Interview. 25 February. 2017.

-----. Personal Interview. 28 February. 2017.

"Modern Art." *The Art Story/Modern Art Insight,* www.theartstory. org/definition-modern-art.htm.

APPENDIX A

An image of *Formation* in its entirety with references to judge size accurately.

Figure 1 *Formation* by Daleene Menning, Grand Valley State University Art Gallery Collection (1998.424.1). Henry Hall, Allendale Campus, 1996.

Many forms of casted objects and impressions are shown, including the keyboard mentioned by Menning.

Figure 2 Detail of *Formation* by Daleene Menning, Grand Valley State University Art Gallery Collection (1998.424.1). Henry Hall, Allendale Campus, 1996.

A close-up of the wall, highlighting the different colors of the tiles.

Figure 3   Detail of *Formation* by Daleene Menning, Grand Valley State University Art Gallery Collection (1998.424.1). Henry Hall, Allendale Campus, 1996.

THE SOUND OF SILENCE

"Music gives a soul to the universe,
Wings to the mind, flight to the imagination,
A charm to sadness, and life to everything" –Plato

Music is synonymous with the creation of humankind; if we could speak, we could sing. From the old Gregorian Plainchants, to new age EDM, music has always been an integral part in our lives. While kids today are exposed to music more frequently, thanks to inventions such as the radio, the ipod, and free streaming services on the internet, most of their first encounters of playing music occur at the elementary education level. It starts with the introduction of the recorder around 4th grade, and then continues with the selection of either band or orchestra in 5th grade. After 5th grade, students may choose to continue playing throughout their educational experience. However, there is a bigger, and more pressing, decision looming than a student's choice between band or orchestra. School districts are cutting funding to music and other fine arts departments, with some districts proposing to get rid of the departments all together.

From an economic and educational standpoint, cutting music education from schools makes sense. Educational programs focus on STEM courses and learning, so fine arts programs like musical education barley get attention as integral parts of the curriculum. By cutting fine arts from the education budget, the money from the department can be allocated to other STEM related courses and resources. This is especially crucial now since the United States is falling behind in these categories. Per the Programme for International Student Assessment (or PISA), in 2015, the U.S. was ranked 38th in math and 24th in science out of 71 countries (qtd. in DeSilver). Supporters of cutting fine arts programs state that the money saved from dissolving the departments will be beneficial towards STEM research, placing the U.S. higher in the rankings over time.

Other supporters question the educational "benefits" that music education claims to have. Kevin O. Davenport of Tennessee State University recently conducted a study comparing middle school students who were enrolled in instrumental music classes to those who were not. In his study, Davenport concluded that there was no significant difference in both GPA and school attendance between the two groups (Davenport 68-69). With this finding, many believe that continuing music education through middle school is a waste of time, money, and resources. Additionally, since there is no significant correlation between GPA and instrumental music enrollment, music education may be seen as a hindrance to a child's education, providing more leverage for its removal.

Although there is evidence that defunding and/or eliminating music education programs has no negative impacts on a student's success, the effectiveness of these arguments deteriorates under closer evaluation. The claim that eradicating music education in schools frees up money in a district's budget is valid, as the removal of any program will save money. However, how much savings would the removal of educational music programs be worth? According to Mark L. Fermanich, not much. In his study, he examines a school district referred to as "Mountain View" which has 70,000 students and an annual operating budget of $900 million (Fermanich 136). This equates to $9,000 a student, which Fermanich states is roughly equal to the national average for a district with more than 15,000 students. Of the $900 million budget, $13.9 million was allocated to music programs (Fermanich 136-37). While $14 million might seem like a lot, that is only 1.6% of the total budget, and 90% of the music program's portions went to solely pay instructors' salaries. These miniscule funding amounts led some music programs, such as marching bands, to rely on their band boosters club to raise up to tens of thousands of dollars separate from the budget to keep afloat (Fermanich 138). Even as it stands today, music programs are underfunded. As a result, 1.6% of a district's budget would not significantly increase students' performance in the areas of STEM enough to justify the removal of music education.

The other argument was that music education does not provide any academic benefits and should be removed in all academic environments. This may be true in lower levels of education (i.e. elementary and middle school) as demonstrated by Davenport's study. However, Davenport's study also monitored high school students who were in instrumental music classes and compared them to those who were not. Surprisingly, high school students enrolled in instrumental music classes scored an average of 15 and 16 points higher in the English and algebra portions, respectively, on the HAS (Maryland high school assessment) than their peers who were not (Davenport 65). In addition, the students who were enrolled attended an average of 2.6 more days in the school year, including days when they were sick in order to participate in rehearsals (67-68). Thus, music education in higher levels of schooling, such as high school, has been shown to increase multiple areas of academic interest and performance for those enrolled. Additional evidence supporting these findings was seen in another study where students enrolled in instrumental music classes had significantly higher CITO-eindtoets-scores than those who were not. The CITO-eindtoets provides a good representation of cognitive functions and a strong predictor of future academic achievements (Knooren 178). In summary, the benefits of being enrolled in music education at the high school level show significant evidence of academic success and cognitive improvement. Cutting music education off at the middle school level is not only detrimental to students, but could also be catastrophic to the educational system that it was believed to be a hindrance to.

The positive cognitive benefits of music education are not just limited to performance in the schools. The cognitive training that occurs from music education can be applied to everyday tasks in the outside world as well. When listening to music, areas from both hemispheres of the brain have been shown to respond to the stimulus. This means that processing networks found in both hemispheres (i.e. language and reading) would then overlap, which has been shown to significantly increase verbal memory (Pack 7). This cognitive increase would then be beneficial in jobs that require attentiveness at meetings, as well as jobs that require daily interpersonal or small group communication. This benefit is simply attributed to listening to music, but what are the benefits of playing an instrument? When playing an instrument, the musician moves, watches the conductor, and reads music, stimulating multiple areas of the brain in both hemispheres. These areas overlap and create a specialized neural system in the brainstem, which is the common pathway for music and speech (Pack 8). This specialized system "... conceivably could help children develop literacy skills and combat literacy disorders" (Pack 8). As a result of these neural overlaps, the corpus callosum that connects the two hemispheres has been shown to increase in density. A denser corpus callosum facilitates activities that use both hemispheres (like reading), while a less dense corpus callosum increases the risk of being diagnosed with attention disorders like ADHD (Bryant). In recapitulation, the lessons that music education teaches can have cognitive benefits both inside and outside the classroom.

Along with the profusion of evidence linking music education to increased cognitive function, music has been shown to help mentally as well. In higher levels of education, music and fine arts are labeled as elective courses, as they are not beneficial to the common core curriculum. Thus, many students enroll in these elective courses to reduce the workload of the school year. However, taking music education as an elective may be beneficial in more ways than one. Students who played and listened to music reported that they felt less stress and became more energized (Rickard 207). With the culmination of these factors, music education could provide the right amount of a "mental break" that students need to get through the school day. Another mental benefit associated with music is the release of dopamine. Studies have shown that rats that were exposed to music for a short period of time had significantly higher levels of dopamine (up to 18% more) than rats that were not (Akiyama and Sutoo 87). This idea of higher dopamine levels due to music can be associated to humans as well. Individuals who listened to music reported feeling, "positive affect states such as happiness or peace" (Rickard 209). By associating these positive factors to school education, it could increase student participation and attendance in addition to reducing possible mental health disorders caused by educational stress.

Lastly, music education classes are unique in their sense of team cooperation. Unlike core classes that are highly based on individual performance, music classes are based around group cohesion, as each student must work with other students to form one band. This team building aspect helps students establish close relationships with each other and helps create friend groups, which makes each student a part of an "in-group". This strong arts foundation helps build, "...creativity, concentration, problem solving, self-efficacy, coordination, values attention and self-discipline among students", all of which are important life skills (Tergerson 18). When an individual is a part of an educational group, there is usually some task or goal that needs to be completed. In music education, this is usually the performance of a piece. With a goal set, members are more motivated to work together to complete the goal and are satisfied when the goal has been reached (Thibaut and Kelley 258). This sense of reward after the goal's completion can help build self-esteem for individual students, as well as teach them a sense of drive or ambition. While other classes may teach students about group cooperation in the form of group projects, music classes constantly reinforce this principle. This is because each music class is team based, resulting in a greater sense of inclusion and awareness of individuals.

Music education never seems to get quite the recognition it deserves. Consequently, many districts are defunding or dissolving the arts to "trim the fat" on their annual budgets. However, music education only accounts for a fraction of district spending. The benefits of music education range from increased scores on state assessments and higher G.P.A.'s, to cognitive advantages and stronger communication and team working skills. Music classes also provide multiple mental benefits, including stress relief and increases in positive moods. As a result, music education provides innumerable and irreplaceable benefits that would be catastrophic to a district and students if cut. If music education is to be removed, there will be no more school concerts, musicals, or tunes that flood the halls from class rehearsals. All that will be left in the music halls is a single sound, silence.

Word Count: 1771

Works Cited

Akiyama, Kayo and Den'etsu Sutoo. "Role of Musical Stimuli in Dopaminergic Brain Function" *Music: Social Impacts, Health Benefits and Perspectives*. By Simon, Peti, and Szabo, Nova Science Publishers, 2013. ProQuest ebrary. http://site.ebrary.com/lib/gvsu/reader.action?docID=10740855&ppg=165.

Bryant, Michelle. "To Cut or Not to Cut – On Cutting Elective Music Education In Public Schools to Conserve funds." *OpEdNews.com*, 2011.

Davenport, Kevin O. "The Effects of Participation in School Instrumental Music Programs on Student Academic Achievement and School Attendance," *ProQuest Dissertations Publishing*, 2010. *ProQuest*, http://Search.proquest.com.

DeSilver, Drew. "U.S. Students' Academic Achievement Still Lags That of Their Peers in Many Other Countries." *Pew Research Center*, 15 Feb. 2017, www.pewresearch.org/fact-tank/2017/02/15/u-s-students-internationally-math-science/.

Fermanich, M. L. "Money for Music Education: A District Analysis of the How, What, and Where of Spending for Music Education." *Journal of Education Finance*, vol. 37 no. 2, 2011, pp. 130-149. Project MUSE, muse.jhu.edu/article/456335.

Knooren, Jan. "The Influence of Music Practice during Primary School on Cognitive Performance. A Cross-Sectional Study Investigating the Correlation of Music Practice and Cognitive Performance." *MaRBLe*, vol. 1, 2011, openjournals. maastrichtuniversity.nl/Marble/article/view/113.

Pack, Victoria. "The Benefits of Including Music in the Elementary Classroom". *MA Project*, Grand Valley State University, 2010.

Rickard, Nikki S. "Music Listening and Emotional Well-Being" *Fine Arts, Music and Literature: Lifelong Engagement with Music: Benefits for Mental Health and Well-being*.

Rickard, Nikki S., and Katrina McFerran, eds. New York, US: Nova, 2011. ProQuest ebrary. http://site.ebrary.com/lib/gvsu/ reader.action?docID=10682978&ppg=81.

Tergerson, Patricia N. The Academic Benefits of Music in Education: Prioritizing Adequate Number of String Classes in Middle School. *MA Project,* Grand Valley State University, 2001.

Thibaut, John W. and Harold H. Kelley. *The Social Psychology of Groups*. John Wiley & Sons, 1959.

EXEMPLARY INDIVIDUAL ESSAYS

We had 33 students nominated to submit portfolios to be considered for the *Guide to First-Year Writing At Grand Valley State University* last year. If we could, we would publish all of them, but we are limited to selecting just a handful.

For this edition, the editors decided that we wanted to include individual essays that stood out from the 99 student essays we read and discussed this year. These four essays were exemplary models of student writing, and we loved reading them, so we wanted you to read them, too.

Mykenzie Hehl's essay, which she wrote for Professor Julie White's class, "Sharps Injuries: What Can Be Done to Minimize the Risks?" has a laser-like focus on a specific issue of safety in the health care industry—sharps injuries—and she uses sources effectively to explain the topic and explore solutions to the problem.

David Rexford's narrative, written for Professor Susan Laidlaw-McCreery's class, "Are You New Here?" takes place in a medical setting, too. In his essay, he reflects with maturity on how his experience as a hospital lab assistant has given meaning to the endless hours he spends studying as a biomedical sciences major.

Julia Sanderlin explores a local Michigan issue in her essay, "Wolves of Isle Royale." As a student in Professor Aiman Meuller's class, Julia focused on the problem of decreasing population of grey wolves on Lake Superior's largest island, and her clearly organized and well-researched essay offers reasonable, interesting solutions to that problem.

Finally, Tyler Kraker, a student of Professor Sarah Slachter, examines traffic patterns in "Around We Go: The Future of Roads," which creatively and effectively advocates for the use of traffic circles at busy road intersections to increase efficiency and decrease accidents.

Mykenzie's Advice for WRT 150 Students

Start early, and work on each one of your papers every week. I find that writing a paragraph at a time worked best for me, I wasn't overwhelmed and my papers came out great at the end of the semester because I was not rushed. Also, get each of your papers checked at the writing center at least three times throughout the semester. Staying organized and diligent is key to getting an A portfolio.

David's Advice for WRT 150 Students

Plan your day around being ready to write, don't force it. Figure out what your "spot" is and use it to your advantage. Picture your topic in your head while you are writing and try to write with these images in mind. Story telling is much more than simply putting information down; it is important to describe your topic in a way that is interesting. The best way to produce an interesting essay is to become interested in the topic yourself as you write. If you have trouble picking a topic, ask some friends what you are passionate about! Often those around us know better than we do what makes us excited.

Julia's Advice for WRT 150 Students

If you are feeling stuck in the writing process, just take a break and leave the paper for awhile. This helped me come back to my papers with a fresh mind and new ideas. One more piece of advice is to have a bunch of people proofread whether it's at the writing center or a parent, this will bring in ideas and critiques that you may have never thought of before.

Tyler's Advice for WRT 150 Students

Find topics that you care about. If you care about what you write about, it will be much more enjoyable for you to write, and for your peers to read.

SHARPS INJURIES: WHAT CAN BE DONE TO MINIMIZE THE RISKS?

Mykenzie Hehl

"I became more cautious, I became more aware, and I became a safer healthcare worker after being stuck," stated my Aunt Erin, a Registered Nurse at Henry Ford Allegiance Health Hospital, who received a sharps injury in the form of a needlestick last year. "I pricked my finger recapping the syringe after drawing up the insulin and didn't even feel the poke." Luckily, she was using a small gauge insulin needle so the risk factor associated with her needlestick was minimal. As soon as she saw the blood on her glove, she knew what had happened. She immediately had a blood draw and filled out a report with her clinical unit leader (Richardson). Being a prospective nursing student, I want to be aware of the risks that will come with my future profession. My goal is to become a neonatal nurse practitioner, meaning not only will I be exposed to these risks, but I will also be handling infants making my risk even higher due to the nature of my intended field of work. Despite the significant protocol on the appropriate way to handle needles, sharps injuries are still a major risk to healthcare professionals. In order to minimize the number of needlesticks that occur in healthcare workers, we must consider why needlesticks are occurring and find ways to prevent them from happening in the future.

According to Anna Riddell, a specialist registrar in infectious disease and virology for the *British Medical Journal*, "a sharps injury occurs when a sharp object such as a needle, a scalpel, bone fragments, or teeth penetrate(s) the skin." Healthcare workers are exposed to these hazards daily and are at high risk for obtaining a sharps injury, usually in the form a needlestick. Moazzam Zaidi, a researcher from the *Ibnosina Journal of Medicine and Biomedical Sciences*, has found that over three million health professionals are exposed to blood and bodily fluids due to sharps injuries every year. Up to eighty percent of those sharps injuries are preventable; however, they are still occurring each year with no significant decrease in number (53). There are numerous factors that explain why sharps injuries are a major problem; some factors include the risk of spreading blood borne pathogens, insurance costs, emotional distress, work environment, and uneven patient-to-staff ratios. Undoubtedly, human error will always play a factor in the risk of sharps injuries and one can only hope that nursing students like myself are aware of how to reduce the risks involved when using sharps. To do this, we must develop effective ways to minimize those said risks.

According to Susan Wilburn, an occupational and environmental health specialist for the American Nurses Association (ANA), easily preventable needlesticks and other sharps injuries expose healthcare workers to over twenty different blood borne pathogens. These blood borne pathogens can cause chronic illness or even death. Wilburn also states that the most common blood borne pathogens that are contracted by sharps injuries are hepatitis B (HBV), hepatitis C (HCB), and HIV. "Research shows that HIV has a 0.3% risk of transmission, HCB has a 2.7-10% risk, and HBV has a 2-40% risk of being transmitted in the United States" (Wilburn). There are different factors that increase the risk of transmission such as the depth of the injury and the device used. For example, a deep puncture injury may affect deeper layers of the skin and may be more serious than a shallow injury. A larger needle may also be more serious than a needle used for giving diabetic patients their insulin, this is because the larger bore needle is bigger in diameter and allows more bodily fluid to pass through during the time of the incident.

Preventing the spread of blood borne pathogens if a needlestick should occur is at the top priority when handling a sharps injury. The biggest concern directly following a needlestick is to make sure the healthcare worker is vaccinated and to ensure that the healthcare worker receives the proper post-anaphylaxis care. There is no vaccine for HCB or HIV; however, there is a vaccine for HBV. States cannot force healthcare workers to get vaccinated, but all states do offer the HBV vaccine if healthcare workers choose to get vaccinated. The United States Centers for Disease Control and Prevention (CDC) developed a workbook used in healthcare facilities to implement a sharps injury prevention program in 2004 that is still being used as a guideline today. It outlines the risks of blood borne pathogens and the policy for dealing with the transmission of diseases. Healthcare facilities should require their staff to read this workbook upon employment. Nursing units should hold monthly meetings to discuss sharps safety. Reading the injury prevention program outlined by the CDC would serve as a reminder to healthcare workers on how to deal with the spread of disease when working with sharps. Enforcing this would help make healthcare workers aware of the importance of getting vaccinated to prevent the spread of disease if a sharps injury should occur. It is important to get vaccinated because although a healthcare worker may never experience a sharps injury in their career; the one time that they might has the potential to affect their entire life.

A contributing factor as to why needlesticks occur despite the protocol in place to prevent them may be due to the work environments and uneven patient-to-nurse ratios. According to a study done by Sean Clarke and his coworkers, a team of doctors in Philadelphia that concentrates their efforts on the study of needlestick prevention, in over twenty-two hospitals across the country nurses had four to nine patients assigned to them on average and were described as having a heavy workload (215). Their findings suggest that "even across hospitals believed to be of better-than-average quality, levels of staffing and variations in work climate are associated with differential needle stick risk," (215). The higher a patient-to-nurse ratio is the more likely nurses are to rush their procedures when handling sharps. The more stressed healthcare professionals are, the less likely they are to think about all the steps pertaining to needle safety while carrying out a procedure. The research conducted shows that rushing a procedure accounts for 47.6 percent of sharps injuries, while carelessness of staff is around forty percent (210). The research also showed that nurses who have been in the field for ten plus years think about needle precautions only sixteen percent daily (211). It is possible that nurses may just be going through the motions without thinking about the specifics, especially if they have done the procedure hundreds of times. Nurses must be especially careful and always be conscious of their surroundings to prevent needlesticks from happening.

My Aunt Erin stated in her interview that on any given day, she may have eight to ten patients assigned to herself alone. "The fact of the matter is, the more patients I have assigned to me at one time, the less opportunity I have to go through every motion in my head about the proper protocol. My priority is getting things done quickly and moving onto the next patient to keep my workload as evenly distributed as possible" (Richardson). Hearing this made me consider possible options to help redistribute the workload among healthcare facilities. Facilities could assign certain room numbers to one nurse every day or assign them a specific wing of the facility to stay more consistent. Healthcare facilities may also benefit from appointing a "floating nurse" during shifts that could pick up the influx of patients on any given day to help distribute the workload more effectively. All units should be posting protocol signs near disposal containers to remind nurses to complete a mental checklist of the proper protocol for their procedures. Of course, it is easier said than done but if healthcare facilities gather as a team and develop stronger game plans to tackle the large patient-to-nurse ratios, stress levels and workloads would decrease, creating a more positive work environment. This would allow more time and focus during patient procedures ultimately leading to lower numbers of sharps injuries.

Despite the different types of sharps management plans, sharps injuries are still being seen in places of high stress due to lack of communication between team members. Carina Stanton, a medical assistant that was published by the *American periOperative Registered Nurse Association (AORN)*, says "three quarters of the estimated 7,000 surgical sharps injuries occurred in the process of handing off or passing sharps during surgical procedures". Although rates of sharps injuries dropped between 1993 and 2000, the rates of sharps injuries occurring in the operating rooms has increased (79). The lack of communication in surgical procedures when passing sharps puts the patient and professionals at risk. If the proper communication is not established healthcare teams are at risk for dropping sharps, grabbing tools from the wrong end, or cutting themselves with the tool they are using. Surgical settings have a fast-paced atmosphere meaning that sharps must be passed quickly in order to be efficient. It is especially important that there is communication between team members in operating rooms and surgical settings because a sharps pass could be detrimental to a staff member or the patient if done the incorrect way.

Tackling this problem can be found in the efforts of AORN. AORN is putting into play a sharps management bundle that will include tools on addressing sharps safety such as creating a neutral zone for passing sharps, the use of sharps safety products, and raising awareness between team members in the operating rooms (80). Deborah Spratt, another member of AORN, says that "nurses alone can't drive widespread adoption of sharps safety practices. Every member of the team must be on board, so that if one member of the team isn't following established safety protocol, other members of the team will remind them what to do." Promoting communication in workspaces and putting these types of practices into play will reduce the number of sharps injuries that occur during surgical procedures. While completing my clinical rotations at Grand Valley State University, I will make it a point to communicate effectively with my team in our simulated labs. This way, I will already have the proper communication skills to prevent things like sharps injuries from occurring. It is important that every member of the team is held accountable for their actions to help keep everyone safe. Being able to have confidence in your team can help prevent injury in surgical settings.

The cost of sharps injuries is one major reason why safer sharps devices need to be more readily available. The CDC's "stops sticks campaign" describes the direct and indirect costs of needlesticks, which include loss of employee time, laboratory testing, post anaphylaxis costs, and the cost of the staff that investigate the injury. Not only do costs effect the healthcare facility but is also affects the emotional state of the employee and the surrounding staff. Post anaphylaxis procedures can take months or even years depending on the severity of the sharps injury. Post anaphylaxis costs include blood testing, vaccines, medications, and counseling for the staff affected. Insurance costs can include paying for an investigator, paying for worker's compensation, and paying other staff members to fill in if necessary. These things all affect the healthcare facilities' integrity and credibility to care for their patients and keep their workers safe.

The only way to lower the cost of sharps injuries is to prevent them from occurring. Because human error will always play a factor, making safer needle sets more available in healthcare facilities is crucial. Some examples of these safer needle devices are needle sets with safety recapping mechanisms or needles that have a sheath to cover them after the device has been used. Using these types of safety devices will help minimize the number of needlesticks that occur post-procedure. Between using safer needle devices, and making sure that sharps containers are close nearby, healthcare facilities can minimize the number of needlesticks and reduce the cost of them if they should occur. It is more cost effective to have the proper devices on hand first, than it is to treat a sharps injury later.

Through investigation, I have become more aware of the reasons why needlesticks are still occurring in healthcare facilities even though safer needle protocols have been put in place.

Exploring the causes for sharps injuries makes me aware of how important it will be to stay conscious of needle safety once I am in my career field. In order to keep myself, my co-workers, and my patients safe, I will need to stay conscious of sharps protocol at all times. Problems with work environments, insurance costs, and risk of spreading disease are all things to be concerned about when dealing with sharps injuries. Human error will always play a factor, but an attempt to reduce sharps injuries healthcare workers must communicate with their teams and be well educated on sharps protocol. It will take a collective effort between all members and branches of the healthcare field, but as medical equipment/training becomes more comprehensive, I am confident that the number of sharps injuries will begin to decrease.

Word Count: 2191

Works Cited

Clarke, Sean P., et al. "Organizational Climate, Staffing, and Safety Equipment as Predictors of Needlestick Injuries and Near-misses in Hospital Nurses." *Association for Professionals in Infection Control and Epidemiology,* June 2002, pp. 207-215. *Science Direct,* doi:10.1067/mic.2002.123392.

Richardson, Erin. Personal interview. 7 Feb. 2017.

Riddell, Anna, et al. "Management of Sharps Injuries in the Healthcare Setting." *British Medical Journal,* July 2015, pp. 1-9. *Academic Search Premier,* doi: 10.1136/bmj.h3733.

Stanton, Carina. "Preventing Sharps Injuries." *Association of periOperative Registered Nurses,* vol. 92, no. 6s, 2010, pp. s78-s80. *AORN Journal,* aorn.org/aorn-journal.

United States, Department of Health, Centers for Disease Control and Prevention. "Stop Sticks Campaign." *The National Institute for Occupational Safety and Health,* 24 June 2011. cdc.gov/niosh/stopsticks/sharpsinjuries.html.

Wilburn, Susan Q. "Needlestick and Sharps Injury Prevention." *The Online Journal of Issues in Nursing,* vol. 9, no. 3, Sept. 2004. *CINAHL Complete,* ebscohost.com/nursing.

Zaidi, Moazzam A., et al. "Needle Stick Injuries: An Overview of the Size of the Problem, Prevention & Management." *Ibnosino Journal of Medicine and Biomedical Sciences,* vol. 2, no. 2, Mar. 2010, pp. 53-61. *Academic Search Premier,* web.b.ebscohost.com/ehost/search/advanced.

"ARE YOU NEW HERE?"

David Rexford

My name is David Rexford. In recent years, rather than David, I am identified to those around me, usually affectionately, as "the guy who studies a lot." School is an immense part of my hopes for my future and I like many other undergraduate medical students who hope to one day be physicians surrounded by people, presently spend most of my days locked in my dark bedroom. In my room I have a $15 single bulb lamp, lit to keep the only area that I should notice illuminated, my desk. While this may seem a repulsive description for most readers, I have grown to greatly appreciate what I can learn about science and hope that my current extraordinary effort will prove valuable to my future patients when I one day accept the intimidating responsibility of being in charge of their health.

In the glorious final week of my freshmen year, I was given a weeklong break from class to study for upcoming exams. Thus far, a descriptive highlight of the week had been one late night my friend Jake and I were studying at the library and suddenly found ourselves in a pitch black room. We had passed unseen in a secluded corner and the building had closed down with us still working inside. This was conclusive proof, we were dedicated. In the midst of these hectic days, the purpose behind my drive for studying showed up on my phone in the form of a call about an open position called a Lab Assistant at North Ottawa Community Hospital in Grand Haven. Craving hospital experience, I jumped at the opportunity, submitting my application about an hour after the call. Regardless of my lack of familiarity with the position, a chance to work in a hospital meant so much to me I would have likely been excited for a shift even if I was simply expected to take out laboratory garbage.

Somehow, I managed to balance my course work, make a drive back home, and show up for a 10am interview on time. After sitting in the Laboratory waiting room for about 20 minutes and getting progressively more nervous, a kind voice called me out of my thoughts and invited me back to an office in the lab where I was, I felt, to be assertively interrogated about every area of my life. In spite of my concerns about the success of the experience, the interview went quite well. I found myself in a room with three, gradually less intimidating, other individuals who had the same expectations for me as I had for myself. The position was an excellent fit for my talents and interests, and, most thankfully, those who interviewed me were also convinced and I was offered the job.

My first several days of work were spent navigating through a significant number of legal documents, reading procedures, and most heavily, learning about the venipuncture procedure. I trained with two other college students, Jake and Paige, who also had similar hopes of being future physicians. The most exciting part of this training was when we were given an artificial arm to enhance our blood drawing skills. The process went like this: tie tourniquet, palpate for a vein, assemble drawing equipment, sanitize draw site, select appropriate tubes, perform venipuncture, slip tubes on in correct order, once blood flow is established (at this point water flow, which was introduced to our practice model's veins from a bag) release the tourniquet, after final tube is filled quickly remove needle and simultaneously cover draw site with gauze and apply pressure. After several days of shying away from every opportunity, I agreed to practice, and I must stress the word practice, drawing blood from one of my coworkers.

The pressure of breaking another human's skin and withdrawing fluid from their circulatory system is doubtlessly intimidating, even more important however, is possessing the ability to stay on task in spite of this pressure. "Is this a good spot?" I asked my coworker, considering a vein that seemed particularly hospitable. "You tell me, you're the one drawing!", she responded playfully. Eventually, ignoring my sweaty, slightly shaky, hands sticking to my gloves, I counted down 3, 2, 1 and poked an undeserving coworker who had been nothing but kind to me with a 22-gauge needle. The draw was successful and perhaps for the first time, I was elated to see blood.

In spite of my success, the most threatening part of the learning process was going into the draw rooms with a coworker who knew what they were doing and attempting to present an attitude of confidence in front of a patient whom I had just met while secretly knowing I had only been drawing from real humans for, in early cases, a few days at best. Throughout the draw, questions would race into my mind. Unfortunately, I was not able to ask for help from whoever was training me, these questions would demonstrate my inexperience to the patient. Characteristic of this job in particular was not only that I was on the spot during the training process but also that patients could not be made aware of this. The apprehensions I carried could not be endearingly shared but had to be withheld to myself.

The first patient I drew blood from was a towering older Dutch gentlemen. Going into the draw room with my coworker, I knew that she was looking for an appropriate patient I could inflict my first draw on, however, neither of us knew when this opportunity might present itself. My trainer recognized this patient as a regular visitor and a rare patient who was not bothered by needles. "David is training with us this summer" she said kindly, "do you mind if we let him draw you today?" The man agreed, rather amused, and with a laugh asked me if this was my first draw. I believe the question was meant to be a joke but, being a new employee, the question had me stumped and I could not think of any way to avoid it outside of blurting out the unfortunate truth as smoothly as I could. "I've drawn from several coworkers, but this will be my first patient draw" I said, with as reassuring of a smile I could muster. Though I would love to recount a beautiful, slick, effortless draw, unfortunately, the draw took its expected place as a rudimentary stepping stone in a training process that I would love to have avoided.

The pressure on phlebotomy trainees is significant. Everyone wants the best "phleb" in the house to draw their blood but, without new employees, capable lab veterans never have a chance to come to life. Even the experienced phlebotomists who have been drawing blood for 30+ years at one point had their first draw, no one is exempt from this unfortunate training process. Training in most areas of the medical field can be more tricky than other fields simply because medical workers carry out their skills on humans rather than things such as machinery or buildings. Even esteemed brain surgeons have their first unassisted surgery experience, one in which they carry out on an individual with a life, friends, family, and coworkers who all wish to see the procedure go smoothly.

At one point during my venipuncture training, I was able to come to a realization that I believe kick started not only my swift success with developing my blood drawing skills, but one that I also trust I will be able to apply down the road in other high-pressure situations. I realized that as I was drawing patients the more confident I was going into the room, the more successful I tended to be. Not only was my success apparent, but I also noticed that patients would feed off of this confidence. It is simple enough to tell a trainee that they must enter the room with confidence and do their job, however, I felt this confidence had no justification. Being new, I was aware that others were much more qualified than I. Coming to the understanding that my own confidence was an imperative part of my success as well as the success of my interaction with patients, I felt better about this sort of "fake it till I make it" attitude. Truly, a negative opinion of myself did not help anyone in the room, and as soon as I made the conscious effort to be positive, I began to focus more of my thoughts on developing my skills, primarily, drawing blood well and simultaneously brightening a patient's day or making them feel more at ease during the procedure.

My experiences following my position at the hospital have honestly been life changing. There are things you might expect, such as getting used to the flow of a hospital, getting to know the staff, and achieving skill in my own area of work, however, there have additionally been many more experiences most would not think of. There are many heartbreaking moments; times when my work shifts from drawing blood to simply sitting down next to elderly patients a few days before their passing and giving them time to express their feelings, or, waiting to be asked to draw blood on a car crash trauma patient in the Emergency Room while looking over the worried faces of family members in the room. There are also happier experiences such as the moments I save the day with my now well represented drawing skills on a patient who is difficult to draw, or, even small things such as making someone laugh who seemed down; not an uncommon experience in a hospital setting. Not only have I learned countless things about healthcare through my work, my duties at the hospital have also opened my eyes to both positive and difficult realities about the world I live in.

Undoubtedly, I have grown to appreciate and enjoy the studying process. I truly have no complaints about my room and my small desk lamp shines light on any and all of my homework with a steadfast devotion, however, I will always favor the fluorescent lights in the ER and most importantly, the faces of patients I am blessed to meet. My study time is directly motivated by my desire to see it later answer the questions of skeptical patients, worried mothers or curious children. As my excitement towards being a future physician grows, I presently work hard to prove myself both at work and at my desk as an approach I can carry with me to my future.

Word Count: 1763

WOLVES OF ISLE ROYALE

Julia Sanderlin

Isle Royale is a magnificent island full of green boreal forests where the impact of humans is extremely limited. It is one of the only places in the world where the animals are not bothered or hunted by humans. Now imagine this island being ravaged by moose, and the beautiful green land becoming barren, giant forests transforming into nothing but shrubbery, and the entire ecosystem starting to die out because all the resources start dwindling. One of the only untouched places on earth would turn in to an island of decay. Sadly, all of this is already starting to happen on Isle Royale because there are no longer enough gray wolves on the island to control the quickly increasing moose population. The gray wolf population has been decreasing at a disturbing rate, and it is now causing a drastic change to the entire environment. More gray wolves should be added to the population for there to be a balance within the environment at Isle Royale. If new gray wolves are not added, then the existing wolves will become extinct due to inbreeding, which will cause the moose populations to rise and forests to turn into savannas.

Isle Royale is the largest natural island in Lake Superior. According to Pat Shipman, ecologists suggested the Natural Park Service to introduce the gray wolves to keep the moose population under control when the park was first founded in 1940. However, the wolves solved that problem themselves by travelling over the ice bridges to the island one winter. The gray wolves are believed to have traveled from Canada to the island in the 1940s. They were able to reach the island because of the ice bridges that form during the winter and connect Isle Royale to Canada (Shipman 341). From then on, the wolves became the only predator and the moose became their only prey. The moose and the gray wolves have been a part of the longest study of predator-prey relationships in an enclosed environment, and this study began in 1958 (Mlot). Researchers from Michigan Technological University have been keeping records and observing the interactions between the wolves and moose annually since then (Spangler).

The gray wolves are an essential part of the environment of Isle Royale in order to keep it balanced. Since the gray wolf numbers have been decreasing, the moose population has been multiplying uncontrollably because there is no longer a top predator to keep their population in check. The herd of moose has now increased to 1,300 (Spangler). If there are no top predators, then the population will keep increasing until they consume all of the vegetation on the island and ruin the ecological environment (Billock). Eventually they will run out of food and the moose will start to starve to death. In the summer months, each moose individually consumes between thirty and forty pounds of vegetation every day and they feed for approximately 8 hours (Vucetich). The gray wolves, to a certain extent, control how the vegetation on the island is distributed by controlling how the moose population is distributed (National Park Service). When there are large herbivores like elk, deer, or moose, there needs to be a top predator to keep the population in check (Billock).

The moose's extreme feeding needs will cause a drastic change on the environment of Isle Royale. According to Michael Rotter, the forests on Isle Royale are already being converted into open woodlands and savannas because of the over browsing moose population. Tree saplings are not able to develop and replace the mature tree before they are consumed by the moose. Therefore, where there once were trees, there are now grasslands and shrubs (Rotter 77). This process is called savannification. Savannification is giving ruderal plant species, which are non-native plants to the island, an opportunity to make their way to the disturbed parts of Isle Royale (National Park Service). This change from forest to savanna will definitely have an effect on the entire ecosystem of the island.

In the 1980s, the population was recorded at its high at 50 gray wolves (Shipman 340). Currently, as of 2017, there are only two wolves left on the island, one male and one female (National Park Service). This decline in the population is likely due to the inbreeding of the gray wolves. The gene pool is too small and it causes health problems to the gray wolves. It is not likely the surviving wolves will be successful in producing viable young and keep the population alive, because they are extremely inbred and it is expected that they would produce young with abnormalities (Shipman 340). The two wolves that remain are the closest related to each other; one is 8 years old and the other is 6 (National Park Service). They are father and daughter as well as half siblings (Mlot).

The pair produced a pup in 2015 and it had visible deformities, but now that pup is believed to be dead; this proves the theory that the wolves would not be able produce healthy pups. in 2017 the female gray wolf showed signs of courtship behavior, but it is not yet known if a pup will be produced (National Park Service).

New gray wolves have not been able to travel to Isle Royale to increase the population because there is no available way for them to reach the island. According to Jennifer Billock, the ice bridges that used to form between Canada and Isle Royale have not been forming due to the rising temperatures. Only two ice bridges have formed in the past 16 years, and this is drastically interfering with the natural gray wolf migration to and from the island (Billock). If the bridges were still forming, new wolves could travel to Isle Royale and strengthen the gene pool (Spangler). During the research of the gray wolf population, researchers found that whenever a new wolf travelled to the island their DNA helped the wolf pack become even stronger. For example, Christine Dell'Amore says in her article, "When a new wolf appeared in 1997... The rejuvenated population hunted more moose in the following decade than ever before." The inbreeding coefficient f dropped in the next few years from 0.81 to below 0.20; 0.00 would be completely outbred and 1.00 would be completely inbred. (Vucetich). This evidence proves that adding additional wolves to the island will correct the extreme inbreeding on the island.

In 2014, the NPS decided against adding new wolves to the Island, but due to the overwhelming comments of people supporting adding wolves, they decided to reintroduce the plan (Mlot). According to the National Park Service, Isle Royale has four different plans to choose between. The first one, also called alternative A, is the no action plan. With this alternative, the national park will not add any wolves or have any interference with the park. However, they will still allow the wolves to immigrate and emigrate from the island as they please. The park will of course still be monitored and all of the environmental changes will be recorded. Including the effect of global warming on the environment (National Park Service).

Alternative B, which is the preferred plan, is the second option. This plan would be started immediately after the decision and it would only last up to five years. The national park would release 20-30 wolves within the first three years. Then after the three years if many of the wolves died, then the park will add more wolves, but only for two more years. The wolves that they plan to capture will be from the Great Lakes area. They will be selecting certain packs, approximately 2-3 packs, that have large genetic diversity along with other individual wolves that will supply even more genetic diversity. The wolves that are selected will all be tested to make sure that they are healthy and will not be bringing any diseases to the island. There are multiple techniques that they may use when capturing the wolves. The one that the National Park Service is most likely to use is a net gun being shot from a helicopter. The wolves will also have limited human interaction so that they do not become habituated to it. The idea with this plan is that there will be enough genetic diversity within the new grey wolf population to last a long amount of time (National Park Service).

Alternative C is the third plan, which entails "immediate introduction, with potential supplemental introductions." This alternative would release only 6-15 gray wolves onto Isle Royale, which is half as many as alternative B suggests. More wolves would later be added to the population as the genetic diversity starts to go down and the wolves need to be rejuvenated. They would continue to add more wolves throughout a twenty-year period as needed. The gray wolf selection and capture would be the same as Alternative B, the only difference being that there would only be 1-2 packs of wolves and a few individual wolves (National Park Service).

Alternative D is the final plan. This plan does not call for immediate action but will allow for action in the future. New gray wolves would be added to Isle Royale under certain conditions. If the moose population increases to 1,500, calf twins observed increase to five total pairs, the moving moose population has a growth rate that exceeds 15 percent. If at least one of those conditions is met, then they will implement a plan that is very similar to alternative C (National Park Service).

The preferred plan, Alternative B, is the favored plan because researchers and the National Parks Conservation Association want to add more wolves in the shortest amount of time possible. This would shorten the amount of time that Park Service will be tampering with the natural environment that many environmentalists believe should stay untouched (Spangler). I think that the best plan would be Alternative C because it is the best plan to solve the genetic diversity problem. If the National Park Service adds many wolves in a short amount of time, they will be more likely to run out of genetic diversity faster because there won't be any new wolves added after the five-year period. By adding new wolves throughout more time the gene pool will keep being replenished, and it will help manage the inbreeding coefficient f to low, healthy numbers that it is supposed to be.

Opponents of the plan to add more wolves would be more in favor of alternative A so that no action will take place and mother nature would be left alone. In Dell'Amore's article, she mentions a senior researcher that works with the U.S. Geological Survey, David Mech, who was a part of the study on the relationship between the moose and the gray wolves when it was first started. Mech believes that the wolf population is not actually affected by inbreeding as much as ecologists are saying. He argues that the gray wolves were still able to successfully hunt the moose. Mech also argued that the population has always been inbred and that the population started off with only one female and two males (Dell'Amore). However, it was proven that inbreeding situation got so out of hand that now the two remaining gray wolves are not able to produce healthy young even though they are still able to successfully hunt moose (Mlot). Even though there were not any noticeable signs of the inbreeding causing defects, in 2009, scientists inspected approximately 50 grey wolf skeletons from Isle Royale, and they found that many had deformations in their spines. These deformities likely caused the wolves to have nerve damage in their tales and hind legs (Vucetich).

The National Park Service reported that there have been public meetings to discuss the plans and which one would be the best route. The commenting period for people on the plans ends on March 15, 2017. In the spring and summer of 2017, the National Park Service will analyze the comments and come up with a Final Environmental Impact Statement, which will be released in the fall/winter of 2017. Finally, whichever plan is chosen will be implemented in the spring of 2018. If the decision is made they will be adding new wolves to the existing population of two. The two remaining wolves will either become a part of one of the added packs or be killed by the new wolves (National Park Service). Either way, the population will be replenished and it will have a positive impact on the environment of Isle Royale (Dell'Amore). In Christine Mlot's article, she says, "Wolves have been successfully moved and reintroduced to other areas, most notably in Yellowstone National Park and in Sweden." This proves that it will likely be a successful transition for the new wolves.

Isle Royale's environment depends on the gray wolves for a successful balance in the ecosystem. The Park Service needs to add more wolves because the current gray wolf population is far too inbred to produce young, the moose population is increasing drastically, and the forest is turning into savannas. Therefore, more gray wolves should be relocated to Isle Royale for the overall survival of both the wolves and Isle Royale itself.

Word Count: 2204

Works Cited

Billock, Jennifer. "Park Service Weighs Whether to Boost Dwindling Isle Royale Wolf Numbers." *Earth Island Journal*, 14 Jun. 2016, http://www.earthisland.org/journal/index.php/elist/eListRead/Park_Service_Isle_Royale_Wolf_Numbers/.

Dell'Amore, Christine. "Should We Save the Wolves of Isle Royale?" *National Geographic*, 26 Apr. 2014, news.nationalgeographic.com/news/2014/04/140427-wolves-isle-royale-animals-science-nation/.

Mlot, Christine. "Extreme inbreeding likely spells doom for Isle Royale wolves." *Science*, 18 Apr. 2016, www.sciencemag.org/news/2016/04/extreme-inbreeding-likely-spells-doom-isle-royale-wolves.

National Park Service. *Draft Environmental Impact Statement to Address the Presence of Wolves*. 2017. Microsoft PowerPoint File.

Rotter, Michael and Alan J. Rebertus. "Plant Community Development of Isle Royale Moose-Spruce Savannas." *Botany*, vol. 93 no. 2, pp. 77, 1 Feb. 2015. *Academic Search Premier*, web.b.ebscohost.com/ehost/pdfviewer/pdfviewer?vid=5&sid=72178003-04f3-4e24-91e2-217254d4a565%40sessionmgr101&hid=118.

Shipman, Pat. "The Fates of Channel Island Foxes and Isle Royale Wolves." *American Scientist*, vol.104 no. 6, pp. 340-341, 1 Nov. 2016. *Academic Search Premier*, web.b.ebscohost.com/ehost/pdfviewer/pdfviewer?vid=3&sid=ffbba72b-88bc-4c38-ae90-d1822d0fea27%40sessionmgr120&hid=118.

Spangler, Todd. "Isle Royale may add 20-30 wolves to keep pack from disappearing." *Detroit Free Press*, 16 Dec. 2016, www.freep.com/story/news/local/michigan/2016/12/16/isle-royale-wolves-michigan/95486866/.

Vucetich, John. "All About Moose." *Wolf and Moose of Isle Royale*, 2017, www.isleroyalewolf.org/overview/overview/moose.html.

---. "All About Wolves." *Wolf and Moose of Isle Royale*, 2017, www.isleroyalewolf.org/overview/overview/wolves.html.

AROUND WE GO: THE FUTURE OF ROADS

Tyler Kraker

We all groan when we look down the road and see the traffic light turn red. Nobody enjoys waiting at intersections, wasting gas and time. Stop signs and traffic lights are the most common types of intersections in West Michigan and in much of the country. People in the U.S. constantly stop at intersections, but in contrast, Europeans rarely stop while driving. Because Europe utilizes traffic circles, otherwise known as roundabouts, traffic can flow consistently without the need to stop. America must add more traffic circles because they are more efficient and safer than our current intersections, which are not only time-consuming, but dangerous.

The city of Grandville and surrounding towns have a growing problem of traffic backups at stoplights. In crowded areas, the time spent at traffic lights can exceed the time a driver drives the speed limit. For example, the corners of 28th Street and Broadmoor Avenue and Lake Michigan Drive and Wilson Avenue are busy and dangerous intersections. These are ones which I deal with often and sometimes wait a full light cycle before getting the opportunity to proceed, which can take up to four minutes. This is a widespread issue for many other people; hundreds, if not thousands, of other drivers must traverse the intersection daily. The effect of a solution would be cumulative with the amount of intersections that could be improved. In addition to the time wasted, these intersections are dangerous. The infamous 28th Street and Broadmoor Avenue intersection has forced the second most crashes, seventy-seven, in 2016. Likewise, Lake Michigan Drive and Wilson Avenue, which ranks number eight of the most dangerous in Kent County, has had sixty crashes last year ("What"). Many of these crashes are caused due to the size of the intersection and busyness of traffic. It is clear to see that there are many problems with stop light intersections.

These standard U.S. intersections pose a serious issue: the safety of the public. Intersections account for forty-five percent of all traffic collisions ("Merry-Go-Round"). Eun-Ha Choi, Ph.D., a contractor from an incorporation working with the National Center for Statistics and Analysis, writes a report that provides a graph illustrating different factors in crashes. He shows that twenty-two percent of all crashes are caused by misjudged left turns at intersections (3). Furthermore, the main reason behind crashes is due to inadequate surveillance by the driver, making up forty-four percent of intersection crashes (6). Additionally, current stoplight intersections find their flaw when the power goes down. Jorge Millian, a journalist in Palm Beach, Florida, describes the situation after Hurricane Irma in respect to the intersections, darkened without their traffic lights. He mentions a story published by *The Palm Beach Post*, which names a specific two intersections in the top ten most dangerous intersections in Florida, which both lost power after Irma. In this situation, the amount of emergency calls due to the recent hurricane withheld officers from directing traffic, leaving the already dangerous intersections without any authoritative guidance (Millian 8). Millian describes the shortcomings of stoplights: "Even with working traffic lights, the intersection can be dicey. Without them, it's a nonstop game of chicken." He says this because the people driving through the area constantly fail to travel through the darkened intersections correctly. Intersections with traffic lights are often dangerous; there must be a simpler solution.

A common substitute for traffic light intersections are roundabouts, but it is evident that the majority of people do not prefer these circular intersections when one asks the public. This is what Retting et al. show in their data, after performing telephone surveys gathering public opinion, and field surveys to observe the change in traffic flow. The results of the public opinion surveys conclude that the majority of people, sixty-nine percent among three states do not support roundabouts to any extent (Retting, et al. 32). The change does not pick up many supporters, but that is changing.

When traffic circles were added in these three states, the data shows the before and after affects, demonstrating that roundabouts improved traffic flow by minimizing delay, and gained public support. Among the states, the average time of vehicle delay decreased by eighteen percent, meaning that cars stopped less, and the percent of cars that came to a complete stop decreased twenty-eight percent. After the roundabouts had been utilized for some time, more telephone surveys concluded that among the drivers who had driven through the new circular intersections, seventy-two percent supported them (Retting, et al. 32). Society seems to never like change; however, once the positive effects are seen, it will be hard to go back.

There is much opposition to the implementation of traffic circles into our road system. Rick Noack, a foreign affairs reporter for the *Washington Post*, quotes Zachary Crockett, a writer from a company called Priceonomics: "The roughly 3700 circular traffic intersections in the U.S. are feared, avoided, and even loathed, often without good reason." The public has many excuses to not favor traffic circles. One hesitation are the many people who do not understand the rules of roundabouts, which can easily be included into the curriculum at driver's training schools, or they simply do not like the change from the normal intersections which they are accustomed to. Additionally, the time that it could take for congested intersections to be converted into a roundabout intersection makes it challenging to implement, disabling the roads that people utilize on a daily basis. Furthermore, the amount of space that a roundabout takes exceeds the area that an average intersection requires. This brings into play the buildings that are close to the intersection, which would be in the way of a potential roundabout. Some of these reasons are valid arguments, but nevertheless, traffic circles are the solution, and they are becoming more popular.

More and more roundabouts are being built around the country, but the U.S. is still falling behind other countries of the world. In European countries, like Britain and France, traffic circles are common, France having twenty thousand alone ("Merry-Go-Round"). In France, one in every forty-six intersections is a roundabout, compared to the U.S., which only has one in every 1118 (Noack). The United States has been adding about one hundred fifty to two hundred fifty new traffic circles every year. In just the state of Washington, the number has gone from seventeen in 2001 to over a hundred in 2007, which accounted for ten percent of the traffic circles in the nation at the time. Many cities are catching on to the effectiveness of traffic circles, even the city of North Pole in Alaska, where one has been added to the corner of St Nicholas Drive and Santa Claus Lane ("Merry-Go-Round"). America is finally beginning to learn that regular intersections are inferior to roundabouts. Even in my community, a few roundabouts have been added. The corner of Wilson Avenue and Remembrance Road has become a traffic circle in the summer of 2015. According to the City of Walker's website, the intersection was changed into a roundabout due to the "complaints of residents for many years." To solve the issue, the city worked with the Michigan Department of Transportation to design and construct a new roundabout ("Wilson"). After driving through it several times, I have seen, first-hand, the evidence that roundabouts are the solution of intersections.

There are many reasons why circular intersections are superior to traditional traffic lights. Revisiting an idea expressed earlier, the shear simplicity of traffic circles defeats the issue of power outages, since there are no traffic signals to power. Furthermore, Noack directs our attention to the Washington State Department of Transportation, who provide us with three reasons how roundabouts save lives, prevent damage, and improve traffic. Since the intersection is now curved, head-on crashes will not be a reoccurring issue. Additionally, drivers must slow down as they approach a traffic circle, decreasing the chance of a collision. Finally, drivers will not be inclined to increase their speed to quickly pass through a traffic light that has become yellow (Noack). They will pass carefully and orderly into the circle, and flow out in their desired direction. In addition to allowing traffic to flow better, roundabouts are safer than the average traffic light intersection. As stated previously, left turns are the primary cause of collisions at intersections, but in the case of roundabouts, there is no such issue. Noack mentions data that comes from a 2001 study done by the American Insurance Institute for Highway Safety, stating that "roundabouts reduced injury crashes by seventy-five percent at intersections where stop signs or signals were previously used for traffic control." This data reinforces the fact that circular intersections are contributing to the overall safety on the roads. In 2006, injuries from all motor-vehicle accidents were reduced by six percent to 2007 ("Merry-Go-Round"). The amount of collisions, damages, and injuries will only continue to decrease with the addition of more roundabouts.

Next time you are sitting in your car, waiting behind a red traffic light, remember that you could have kept moving, but without the increase of traffic circles, you cannot. With more traffic circles, drivers would keep moving at a higher rate. The community must face the fear of change, and embrace the solution to our problem. Traffic circles are the answer since they have been proven to be more effective for traffic flow and safer than the current intersections. No longer will anyone be forced to stop at another dreaded red light when traffic circles are implemented in our community, and across the country.

Word Count: 1589

Works Cited

Choi, Eun-Ha. "Analysis and Results." *Crash Factors in Intersection-Related Crashes: An On-Scene Perspective*, National Highway Traffic Safety Administration, September 2010, pp. 2-20, crashstats.nhtsa.dot.gov/Api/Public/ViewPublication/811366, Accessed 8 November 2017.

"Merry-Go-Round; The Boom in Roundabouts." *The Economist*, 11 August 2007, p.24. *Infotrac Newsstand*, go.galegroup.com/ps/i.do?p=STND&sw=w&u=lom_gvalleysu&v=2.1&id=GALE%7CA167393659&it=r&asid=6b8ddb6205c742be553715d88bfff3d8, Accessed 1 November 2017.

Millian, Jorge. "Traffic Light Out at Two of Worst Intersections." *Palm Beach Post [West Palm Beach, FL]*, The Atlantic Journal Constitution, 14 September 2017, p. 8. *Infotrac Newstand*, go.galegroup.com/ps/i.do?p=STND&sw=w&u=lom_gvalleysu&v=2.1&id=GALE%7CA504453778&it=r&asid=5f8593a31af7c5b043c0cc0427c6c0dc, Accessed 7 November 2017.

Noack, Rick. "Americans Don't Like Roundabouts, but They Should." *Washingtonpost.com*, 17 March 2016. *Infotrac. Newsstand*, go.galegroup.com/ps/i.do?p=STND&sw=w&u=lom_gvalleysu&v=2.1&id=GALE%7CA446615437&it=r&asid=b603e3f7e906e1824e0df7643112e621, Accessed 1 November 2017.

Retting, Richard A, et al. "Public Opinion and Traffic Flow Impacts of Newly Installed Modern Roundabouts in the United States." *ITE Journal*, Vol. 72, Iss. 9, Institute of Transportation Engineers, September 2002, pp. 30-33. *ProQuest*, search.proquest.com/docview/224882576/fulltext/A669CD787B594279PQ/1?accountid=39473, Accessed 7 November 2017.

"What are the High Crash Intersections in Grand Rapids, Michigan?" *Michigan Auto Law: Auto Accident Attorneys*, www.michiganautolaw.com/firm_profile/attorney-locations/grand-rapids-dangerous-intersections/, Accessed 8 November 2017.

"Wilson (M-11) / Remembrance Roundabout." *City of Walker*, www.walker.city/business/city_projects/wilson_remembrance_(m-11)_roundabout_(mdot).php, Accessed 29 November 2017.

The Department of Writing offers a curriculum that teaches students to construct texts that appeal to different audiences, a critical skill for the 21st century. With the proliferation of online and accelerated communication, the ability to tell a story that engages and persuades an audience is more important than ever. A degree in writing can help students develop these skills.

Writing majors and minors will have opportunities to develop storytelling skills in a wide variety of genres and media. Whether students are interested in connecting storytelling to traditional genres (academic, poetry, magazine, fiction, non-fiction) or to the latest writing technologies (document design software, content management systems), they can select courses that best prepare them for future professional careers.

Through a unique modular curriculum that combines courses in professional, academic, and creative writing, students will learn how to create, shape, design, and share texts. These abilities will allow them to enter the world in a variety of careers such as Web writer, freelancer, document designer, magazine writer, editor, publisher, or technical writer, to name a few. The flexibility and the variety of courses offered lets students shape their educational experience and future professional identity.

Through the BA or BS degree, writing majors develop the skill set to:

- ▶ Write fiction and non-fiction texts.
- ▶ Develop and tailor content to both print and online media.
- ▶ Work with the industry standard writing and design software.
- ▶ Collaborate with other writers, editors, subject matter experts, and designers to prepare content for publication.
- ▶ Develop promotional materials to pitch and sell content.

Christopher Toth, Chair
Professor of Writing
Lake Ontario Hall 326
Department of Writing
616-331-3411
www.gvsu.edu/writing

GRAND VALLEY STATE UNIVERSITY.

licensing through Learfield Licensing Partners (http://learfieldlicensing.com/licensing/)